Optimal Nutrition

RAW AND COOKED CANINE DIETS:
THE NEXT LEVEL

Monica Segal, AHCW
Foreword by Ana S. Hill, DVM, PhD

Note to the reader: This material has been written and published for educational purposes and is not intended to replace the advice of your veterinarian. Readers acting on this information do so at their own risk with full knowledge that a veterinarian should be consulted for advice. Neither the author nor publisher have responsibility or liability to any pet, person, or entity with respect to damage, loss or injury caused or said to be caused directly or indirectly by the information provided herein.

Design, production and editorial services: Triadicon, Inc., Fairfield CT, USA

Cover illustration: Ken Ottinger
Signed 8" x 10" fine art prints are available from the artist at: knlottinger@commspeed.net

Editor: Lindsay Spielmann
Technical Editor: Susan G. Wynn, DVM

First edition, 2007
Published by Doggie Diner, Inc., Toronto, Canada
www.monicasegal.com

Printed in Canada
Transcontinental Printing, Sherbrooke, Québec, Canada

Library and Archives Canada Cataloguing in Publication
Segal, Monica Optimal Nutrition : raw and cooked canine diets / Monica Segal. – 1st ed.
Includes index.
ISBN 978-0-9730948-1-7
1. Dogs--Food. 2. Dogs--Nutrition. 3. Dogs--Health. I. Title.
SF427.4S443 2007   636.7'085   C2006-906974-3

In memory and honor of my mother, Tina Segal.

Table of Contents

CHAPTER 14

CHAPTER 15

CHAPTER 16

CHAPTER 17

CHAPTER 18

PREFACE
Acknowledgements

M Y THANKS AND GRATITUDE go to everyone who supported this book and gave so freely of their time and of themselves. There are too many people to mention, but the following deserve special thanks:

Morley Fruchtman – thank you for cups of tea at midnight, putting up with insane hours every day of every week, cranky moods and sleep-deprived nights. Mostly, thank you for being more than any workaholic wife has a right to expect.

Dad – your support and strength are appreciated more than words can express. Thank you for having faith in me, and never demanding anything more than my best effort.

Ana Hill, DVM, PhD – my good fortune was sealed by having you as part of the team, teacher and support system.

Susan G. Wynn, DVM – my friend, teacher and mentor.

Mike Cormier, DVM – for putting up with never ending questions from this very high-maintenance client. Thanks for your guidance and belief in me.

Heidi Schmeck – your support, creativity, vision and enthusiasm — even under pressure — are so greatly appreciated.

Lowell Halvorson – our imaginative, supportive, driving force with a wonderful sense of humor. Thank you for your generosity throughout the years.

Lindsay Spielmann – thank you for your expertise. Your time, generosity and enthusiasm are appreciated more than I can say.

Caroline Spielmann – one seminar brought a very special friend into my life. Sincere thanks for your wonderful moderation skills on the K9Kitchen list and the support you have given me to allow time for writing.

Janis Mattson, Hazel Olbrich and Lynda Britchford – thanks for the time you devote to the K9Kitchen list. Your help and support are greatly appreciated.

Laura and Ken Ottinger – your friendship is no Cavalier matter.

All the wonderful animals that have taught me about their individual needs — you have all been my teachers.

To the greatest of them all, our Angel Zoey, and the legacy that lives on with this book.

PREFACE
Foreword

YOU LOVE YOUR DOG! I know you love your dog because you're reading this book. People who really love their dogs want to do everything
right for them, everything that's best. People who love their dogs research
breed and temperament, grooming and nutrition, toys and treats, and so
on. Did I say nutrition? Yes! — and that is the focus of this book. People
who love their dogs also care deeply about what they feed these precious
companions. And that includes you!

Monica Segal has worked long and hard to bring you practical
information about feeding your dog carefully and correctly, especially
if you want to home-prepare your animal's food. She describes nutrition
needs for all life stages and for several common medical conditions and
physical situations, along with practical recipes you can prepare in your
own kitchen. She brings you these gems wrapped up in a delightful and
entertaining story of one canine family, Noah and Ally with her puppies,
and their companions. This is not dry reading, my fellow dog lovers!

If you have already read Monica's first book, *K9 Kitchen,* you know
that she does her nutrition homework thoroughly to bring you information and facts, along with origins of myths and nonsense that have worked
their way into feeding practices for pets. She diligently and boldly provides
you with referenced information and adds her own opinions, sharpened
by years of experience as a loving dog owner. Monica home-prepares
food for her animals and has practical experiences to share with you
because she's been there, right in the kitchen, with her dogs at her feet.
She continues to emphasize that every dog — your dog — is an individual
and every dog's diet deserves personalized care and consideration.

I had the pleasure of getting to know Monica nearly 10 years ago, when she contacted the nutrition service where I worked, and asked for advice about recipes she found for her dogs. We worked together on diet plans for her pets and dove into many long, delightful conversations about feeding dogs from puppyhood into old age. My own credentials include a degree in veterinary medicine and a Ph.D. in small animal nutrition, both earned from the University of California, Davis. I have worked with pets and their owners in private practice and in university veterinary referral practices. Working for some years in the commercial pet food industry provided me with valuable information to balance out my experiences in practice and academia. Now as a professor at the Ohio State University, I teach students about animal nutrition and welfare, and I continue to consult with owners who want to home-prepare food for their pets. I feel strongly that pets can benefit from owner-prepared foods if these recipes are well-balanced, made with safe ingredients, and meet the animal's needs at their particular life stage and medical condition (if any).

As you read each chapter and get to know Noah, Ally, and her puppies on their nutritional journey, you will recognize information you can use at home for your own dog. Every recipe and diet plan was reviewed by me and found to meet requirements and be well-balanced for life stage or health conditions. Every recommendation is built on sound nutritional knowledge and Monica's clear interest in the health and welfare of the animal you love so much — your dog. Enjoy!

Ana S. Hill, DVM, PhD
Columbus, Ohio, USA

CHAPTER 1
Introduction

THE HEALTH OF OUR DOGS is a result of many events, some of which occurred before the dog was even born. Genetics, environment and diet are all critical components.

Good breeders know that a careful breeding program, aimed at producing sound dogs that can improve the breed, is a goal that can be achieved over time. A breeding program can be full of surprises even when we attempt to make all the right decisions.

Pet buyers are usually encouraged by ethical breeders, fanciers and veterinarians to investigate a favored breed and become well aware of possible genetic problems prior to purchase. Still, even with information in hand, pet buyers may also end up with a surprise. The puppy that comes from a long line of cancer-free dogs despite his breed being prone to cancer may still end up with a thyroid irregularity, gastrointestinal problems or many other health issues. None of us remain healthy for a lifetime — dogs included.

Discussions about genetics are beyond the scope of this book. However, there are many good sources that you might want to read in order to better understand the challenges and how they may be addressed. In particular, articles written by the award-winning author, respected breeder and immunologist, Susan Thorpe Vargas, PhD, are a good place to begin.

Environment is something that most of us can control to a point by providing clean water sources, using fewer chemicals in our homes, fewer pesticides in our environments, and controlling diet, which is the focus of this book.

Readers are encouraged to read the entire book despite the fact that, as a pet buyer, you may not think that feeding of the pregnant bitch applies to you. In fact, the health of your puppy's mother is very important. You should know what the sire and dam have been eating, and you should ask the breeder about any food sensitivities that either has displayed in the past. The old adage about the apple not falling far from the tree applies in many cases of food allergies or sensitivities.

A healthy diet for a breeding dog is the same as for a pet. The only major difference lies in the needs of a pregnant or lactating bitch. While the breeding dog may use certain nutrients for varying purposes that do not apply to pets, a pet dog deficient in these same nutrients, will also have problems. Therefore, material in this book that at first glance may seem to apply only to breeders is important for those of us feeding pets as well. In addition, all sections of the book contain general information that is necessary to better understand the chapters that follow.

As a breeder, you will want to know what potential pet buyers intend to feed your puppies whether their new destination is a companion or competition home. You will also want to offer mentoring support to new buyers and suggest ways that their new pup can be raised on a home-prepared diet if you prefer non-commercial food.

A key point to consider is that a diet that worked for the breeder may not work for the pet buyer (I receive a lot of mail about this problem). If you want the pet buyer to continue feeding home-prepared foods, chances are that you will need to be able to offer reasonable alternative dietary suggestions.

As passionate dog lovers, both breeders and pet buyers want to be able to feed their dogs (bitches, sires, new pups, growing puppies, canine athletes, show dogs and "senior citizens") optimally and with confidence throughout their lives. If disease occurs, we need to be able to change the diets accordingly. Concurrent diseases present even greater challenges.

This book is a second building block for more complete discussion of the individual needs of dogs from gestation to geriatrics. My first book, *K9Kitchen – Your Dogs' Diet: The Truth Behind The Hype,* discusses a variety of feeding programs, supplements, and the basic interactions of minerals as well as amino acids. It also includes cooked and raw individual diet plans.

Both books aim to provide information you can use to help your dog. I hope that the two books combined will be resources that you can count on during all life stages.

You are about to meet a hypothetical canine family based on some cases I have worked with. Just as your dog is an individual, these family members are unique and serve only as examples of what can occur over a lifetime.

Monica Segal, AHCW
Toronto, Ontario, Canada

CHAPTER 2
Feeding Options

I N MY FIRST BOOK, *K9Kitchen – Your Dogs' Diet: The Truth Behind the Hype,* we discussed the basics of home-prepared diets. We navigated the maze of commercial diets and cooked and raw food choices. You now have a foundation on which you have built a diet plan for your own dogs. The book you are currently reading builds on the information you already have. However, some readers may appreciate a quick refresher of a few basic points from the first book.

Commercial Diets

Many, but not all, commercial diets are based on the guidelines set by the Association of American Feed Control Officials (AAFCO), a regulatory body comprised of government officials from each state who monitor animal feeds sold in their state. The pet food companies have liaisons that go to the AAFCO meetings and try to work with the AAFCO on regulations. Commercial foods formulated to meet AAFCO guidelines are labeled as "complete and balanced."

The old adage "you are what you eat" is probably better expressed as "you are what you absorb." Absorption of nutrients is a complicated process, and a diet that claims to be complete and balanced may or may not meet individual needs. Dr. Quinton Rogers of the University of California, Davis, is a highly respected authority on canine nutrition. Dr. Rogers has stated, "There is very little information on the bioavailability of nutrients for companion animals in many of the common dietary ingredients used in pet foods. These ingredients are generally by-products of the meat, poultry and fishing industries, with the potential for a wide variation in nutrient composition. Claims of nutritional adequacy of pet foods based on the current Association of Feed Control Officials (AAFCO) nutrient allowances ("profiles") do not give assurances of nutritional adequacy and will not until ingredients are analyzed and bioavailability values are incorporated."[1]

We need to ask ourselves, if indeed we were capable of providing optimal nutrition for animals, why would we not do the same thing for people? Bags and cans labeled "child," "adult" and "senior" could easily replace the fresh-food sections in supermarkets. We would have convenience and save money at the same time. Of course, this seems unreasonable given what we know about the healthful properties of fresh foods. Only animals in human care are expected to eat highly processed foods for a lifetime. Emotional arguments aside, there are a number of factors to be considered here.

Mineral Interactions

Minerals interact constantly and greatly affect each other. For instance, excess calcium makes zinc less available to the body, and as I have pointed out, you are what you absorb rather than what you ingest. Zinc plays an important role in immune function and skin health. Copper and zinc also interact as do iron and zinc, calcium and phosphorus, potassium and sodium — and the list goes on! These interactions need to be considered for the health of your dog and the formulation of diets. Poor sources of minerals in some commercial diets may create problems.

For example, zinc oxide is a form of zinc that does little more than enrich the stool. Very little of it is absorbed by the body. Because copper and zinc interact, the amount of copper storage in the body can increase when a poor source of zinc is included in the diet. Excess copper is toxic and can do serious damage to the liver.

There are too many possibilities to list, but it should be clear that the source of a mineral plays a key role. If absorbable supplements are included in the right proportions, home-prepared diets do not have these problems.

Label Claims

Labels can be misleading. Dogs can digest well-cooked grains, but the protein quality of grain is much lower than that in meat. Despite this, the protein content listed on a label includes protein from grain.

---

1   Morris, J.G., Rogers, Q. (2002) Personal conversations.

By law, the ingredient list on the label must state ingredients by order of weight. A label listing chicken, rice, oats, corn, carrots and zucchini simply tells us that the chicken weighs more than any one of the other ingredients. A meat source may be listed first, but there may be more grain in the diet than there is chicken.

Claims of diets passing feeding trials may sound impressive, but the reality of these trials leaves room for doubt. The criteria for a maintenance diet to pass a feeding trial are:

a. All dogs in the test group must be more than one year old.

b. The group consists of eight dogs that are healthy and of normal size and weight.

c. Blood tests are performed at the beginning and end of the feeding trial.

d. The test group must eat only the food being tested.

e. By the end of the testing period, dogs must not have lost more than 15% of their original body weight.

f. During the trial period, no dog may die or need to be removed from the trial due to nutritional causes of illness.

g. Of the original eight dogs, six must complete the test.

h. The feeding trial is 26 weeks in length.

According to the above information, it would not be a problem for a dog that weighed 100 pounds at the beginning of the feeding trial to lose 15 pounds in six months. Most people would be running to their veterinarian if this happened at home! As to nutritional causes of illness, it might be difficult to assess this particular criterion since dogs are highly adaptable animals. Nutritional causes of disease may show up years in the future rather than during a 26-week period. Further, there are some signs that may be ignored by some veterinarians. Hypothyroidism and allergies, to name only two possibilities, may not always be attributed to a faulty diet but can certainly be augmented or worsened by poor nutrition.

Chapter Summary

- Diets may be "complete and balanced" on paper but actual bioavailability of nutrients cannot be assured.
- Mineral interactions affect the final product and absorption by the animal.
- Nutrient absorption varies between individuals and can be hampered or increased to excess levels by mineral interactions, disease factors, genetics, etc.
- Pet food is formulated to meet average requirements.
- The amount of protein in any diet includes proteins found in grains.
- A label stating a meat source as the first ingredient may not mean that meat is the most abundant ingredient in the food.
- Animals under human care are the only creatures expected to thrive on a lifetime of canned and bagged foods.

CHAPTER 3
The Boy

NOAH IS FOUR YEARS OLD and weighs fifty pounds. He was raised on a home-prepared, raw diet and looks to be the picture of health. As a matter of fact, Noah looks so good that he is a favorite in the show ring. However, he is being discussed in some breeding circles because he seems to sire small litters and has failed to impregnate a number of bitches altogether.

While some fault may lie with the bitches, it seems that Noah has been paired with several bitches that have always had large litters in the past. They also had large litters with other dogs after Noah was used so fingers are pointing squarely at him.

Noah's breeder has been very careful to provide a great deal of variety in the diet. Since the dog has an "iron clad" stomach, he eats and enjoys all foods. Below is an example of what Noah ate over a one-week period when he was a puppy and continues to eat today:

Unbalanced Diet

36 ounces chicken necks

10 ounces lamb rib

42 ounces turkey necks

8 ounces mackerel, canned, drained

8 ounces ground beef, raw, lean, 15% fat

12 ounces chicken, dark meat with skin, raw, boneless

4 ounces chicken liver, raw

4 eggs, raw, without shells

1 teaspoon cod liver oil
3,500 milligrams wild salmon oil
4 ounces yogurt
16 ounces mixed green vegetables
1 small apple
16 ounces sweet potato
6 ounces cottage cheese
1 teaspoon kelp
2 teaspoons alfalfa
1,400 IU vitamin E

Obviously, when he was a young puppy, Noah ate smaller amounts of these foods; however, the ingredients are the same. A diet analysis shows the following results:

- This diet provides more than triple the required amounts of calcium and phosphorus.
- The iodine content is greater than is considered healthy for the thyroid gland.
- There are also gross deficiencies of copper, iron, manganese, potassium and zinc.

Deficiencies

Note that, amongst other problems, the zinc deficiency is of particular concern in Noah's case because zinc is linked to sperm production.

How could Noah be deficient in zinc when his diet is obviously so diverse? Would it not balance over time? Unfortunately, deficiencies may be caused by too much variety. Let me explain.

A dog is only able to consume so many kilocalories before he becomes overweight. A 50-pound dog with average activity level consumes 1,000 – 1,200 kilocalories a day. When there is a great deal of variety in the diet, there may not be enough of a nutrient. For instance, a 50-pound dog requires 21 milligrams of zinc per day. This would be provided by 17 ounces of ground beef that contains 15% fat. Zinc is available in other foods; however, beef is very high in zinc so we would require less of this food than of many others. Even so, this amount of beef provides approximately 1,044 kilocalories. Therefore, if a dog consumes enough beef to meet his zinc requirements, we have little to no caloric room left for other foods. The dog would be eating an all-meat diet lacking in other important minerals.

In light of this example, consider that a diet with a great deal of variety would include less beef because it would be "diluted" with other foods. As a result, a zinc deficiency is not only possible but also very likely.

If you have been feeding a highly varied diet like the one above, try the following diet plan instead to correct the imbalances.

Balanced Diet

2 ounces chicken neck

14 ounces turkey neck

3 ounces lamb rib

24 ounces beef heart

3 ¼ ounces beef liver

30 ounces ground beef, lean, 15% fat

36 ounces ground turkey

3 large eggs without shells

1 teaspoon cod liver oil

7,000 milligrams wild salmon oil

6 ounces yogurt, whole milk

16 ounces broccoli

2 small apples

32 ounces sweet potato

½ teaspoon kelp

2 teaspoons alfalfa powder

7 capsules, vitamin E 200 IU

6 capsules, Allergy Research Multi-Vi-Min® without copper and iron[2]

15 milligrams zinc citrate or gluconate

This diet provides 898 kilocalories that break down as 37% from protein, 20% from carbohydrates and 43% from fat.

---

2   Multi-Vi-Min® is a brand name for a vitamin and mineral supplement made by Allergy Research/ Nutricology. It is available in some stores and online.

The supplements noted provide the following nutrient profiles. Look at the details and be sure to purchase items that offer comparable values:

· Kelp: 750 mcg of iodine per ¼ teaspoon

· Cod liver oil liquid (1 teaspoon): 3,750 IU of vitamin A and 375 IU of vitamin D

· Wild salmon oil: Not to be confused with regular salmon oil. The latter is derived from farmed fish, which as headlines have reported for years, contain a load of PCBs and Mercury.

· Vitamin E: This is natural vitamin E, also called d-alpha tocopherol. We would need more of the synthetic version, known as dl-alpha tocopherol, to achieve the same benefits.

Understanding the Changes

You will notice that the new diet plan is not much different from the original, but the changes made are critical. Eliminating chicken necks frees up more calories to be applied towards increased amounts of beef heart and ground beef; more nutrient dense foods. Beef liver, rather than chicken liver, provides a larger amount of copper. The increased amount of sweet potato provides more potassium, manganese, copper and iron. Eliminating the cottage cheese and mackerel reduces the sodium content and provides more caloric room for the above additions.

Any dietary changes must take place within certain caloric parameters. In this case, our revised diet plan provides about the same kilocalories as the original. Still, despite the changes, the diet falls a little short on a few minerals, most noticeably potassium and manganese. To bring the diet up to better levels of all minerals, the addition of the multi-mineral formulation becomes necessary. This may not be necessary if Noah could eat more food without gaining weight.

Perfect Nutrition

Nobody knows what perfect nutrition is, whether for animals or humans. We certainly have some strong opinions about the subject, but if we remain emotionally unattached to the discussion, we see that there are many sides to the story. In fact, optimal nutrition for a dog with one specific disease may be quite different from optimal nutrition for a dog with a different disease, or one that is in great health. This still does not present the whole picture, as dogs may have different food tolerances, energy levels, living conditions, genetic predispositions and caloric requirements.

To better understand arguments about what constitutes the best diet for a dog, we first need to understand the three main schools of thought on the subject:

1. Dogs come from wolves, and wolves eat whole prey animals. Thus, using Mother Nature as a guide, we should feed our dogs whole prey animals (either as whole animals or in pieces that include bones) and perhaps some vegetables and/or grains. The addition of vegetables or grains depends on what various camps believe regarding whether dogs require these foods and whether they make use of their nutrients. Some say that the natural diet of carnivores does not include these foods, and that studies prove that dogs, other than pregnant or lactating bitches, have no need for carbohydrates. However, this point is debated.

2. Dogs have been our companions for thousands of years and have survived to reproduce well while sharing human food. Before commercial diets became available, dogs ate our cooked foods, perhaps supplemented with raw foods found during scavenging.

3. Under the National Research Council (NRC), recommended allowances for dogs, based on scientific studies, have been established. All canine diets — raw, cooked or commercial — should be formulated to meet these numerical values for healthy nutrient intake.

Obviously, these belief systems may clash. The first uses Mother Nature as a guide and does not consider scientific findings in a controlled setting. The second is based on the experience of past generations. One or both of these ideologies may prove to be correct, but a particular diet alone has not been shown to be responsible for multiple generations of domestic dogs reproducing well and living longer, healthier lives. In fact, due to more advanced medicine, more veterinarians and quick medical interventions, dogs live longer lives than in the past, despite consuming canned and bagged foods. In the last belief system, science holds a more important place and the value of each nutrient to be provided in the diet is measured against what researchers are recommending.

Another way of looking at this is that we have progressed or refined feeding methods. Wild dogs ate whole animals, parasites, dirt, gut bacteria and diseased tissue. They lived long enough to reproduce but had to deal with predation, starvation, parasites and disease. Whether or not they met their nutritional needs optimally is debatable. Domestication brought scraps of food that people shared, that were edible for the most part, more free of dirt, and the cooking often reduced the parasite and bacterial load. Dogs no longer had to hunt for food and be at the mercy of predation, starvation and parasitism; however, since breed development was in its infancy, nutritional requirements had yet to be worked out. Enter NRC and then AAFCO (American Association of Feed Control Officials) with thousands of research studies and observations. Now that canine nutrition had been recognized at this new level, it would be better able to better meet animals' needs by species and breed.

Personally, I believe that there is a middle ground to explore. In fact, I think that the belief systems I have noted above can come together nicely. For instance, a report titled "Nutrient Composition of Whole Vertebrate Prey" shows that whole prey meets or exceeds the nutrient requirements of dogs as set by the NRC of 1985[3].

My experience shows that various feeding methods (based on whole prey or published guidelines) can work, but individual dogs need to be considered. Some simply cannot tolerate a raw diet or much fat, or do not have consistent stool without grains in the diet, etc.

Our belief systems are only as viable as our dogs' tolerance of a feeding method. Since my work involves canine diets for many individual problems, I need to find many solutions. To do this, I need to understand the nutrient content of diets by working with NRC guidelines.

The diet analyses and corrections in this book are based on the NRC 2006 guidelines. If I were using strictly the whole prey model of feeding as my guide, I would not be able to correct a diet as I do here (other than by guessing at the problem and solution).

The Rest of The Story

Pet owners with neutered dogs need not worry about sperm production but should note that zinc also plays a critical role in immune system function, skin health and protein synthesis. Zinc deficiency has also recently been found to play a role in diseases associated with diarrhea.

Breeds may vary in their ability to absorb a nutrient. Huskies and Malamutes, for example, can have a genetic predisposition that decreases their ability to absorb zinc.

---

3   Dierenfeld, E. S., Alcorn, H. L., Jacobsen, K. L. (May 2002) Nutrient Composition of Whole Vertebrate Prey (Excluding Fish) Fed In Zoos.

Is there anything that can help Noah at this point? It is difficult if not impossible to change the end result of a poor puppy diet that results in sperm problems. Vitamin E, an antioxidant, has the ability to decrease free radicals and prevent damage to sperm cells.[4,5] Zinc supplementation, under the supervision of your veterinarian, may raise testosterone levels and sperm production.[6]

Finally, note that investigations headed by Dr. Robert Cousins[7] demonstrate that microminerals (also known as trace minerals) could influence the transfer of genetic information and regulation of gene expression. This has tremendous potential impact for all of us but especially so for breeding dogs.

Questionable Outcomes

Minerals interact with each other in many ways. These interactions cause fluctuations in the status of a mineral at any given time. Noah's original diet as a puppy, lacked zinc to begin with, and was also impacted by the fact that calcium binds zinc. Since puppies have poor ability to regulate calcium, the dietary deficiencies may have been even greater than they appear at first glance. In turn, this dog may have suffered other nutrient deficiencies and/or excesses that may display themselves as any number of diseases or conditions over a lifetime. For the breeder, this could be a puzzling surprise since Noah's ancestors were a healthy lot.

This impacts not only Noah's breeder but also raises questions from other breeders and puppy buyers. For instance, if Noah were diagnosed with a thyroid problem, every breeder who bred a bitch to him might be concerned. But think carefully about the iodine content of this dog's original diet. Iodine excess causes changes in thyroid activity. Remember that as a puppy, Noah's diet included a great deal of kelp that provided an enormous amount of iodine. Increased dietary iodine alters thyroid

4   Rolf, C., Cooper, T. G., Yeung, C. H., Nieschlag, E. (April 1999) Antioxidant treatment of patients with asthenozoospermia or moderate oligoasthenozoospermia with high-dose vitamin C and vitamin E: a randomized, placebo-controlled, double-blind study. *Human Reproduction*; 14(4): 1028-1033.

5   Kessopoulou, E., Powers, H. J., Sharma, K. K., Pearson, M. J., Russell, J. M., Cooke, I. D., Barratt, C. L. (Oct 1995) A double-blind randomized placebo cross-over controlled trial using the antioxidant vitamin E to treat reactive oxygen species associated male infertility. *Fertility and Sterility*; 64(4): 825-831.

6   Netter, A., Hartoma, R., Nahoul, K. (1981) Effect of zinc administration on plasma testosterone, dihydrotestosterone and sperm count. *Archives of Andrology*; 7 (11): 69–73.

7   Cousins, R. J., Boston Family Professor of Human Nutrition at the University of Florida, Gainesville.

structure and function in puppies younger than three months old.[8] The end result is a dog with thyroid problems. His breeder could choose to eliminate him from a breeding program. Past breeders and pet buyers would then test their puppies to see if Noah had passed on this problem to his puppies. In reality, Noah's diet (not genetics) could be at fault.

Certainly, genetic flaws do exist. It would be simplistic to suggest that diet alone can impact genetic expression. However, it may be equally simplistic to suggest that it has no effect. Good breeders, making ethical choices in a breeding program, can indeed contribute to genetic expression through diet.

Chapter Summary

· Puppy diets can impact health dramatically for a lifetime.

· Zinc-deficient diets can be the cause of weak sperm as well as affecting immune function, protein synthesis, skin and bowel health.

· A diet that provides a great deal of variety of foods may nevertheless offer incomplete nutrition over the long term.

· Breed predisposition should be considered. For instance, some breeds have a genetic predisposition that decreases their ability to absorb zinc. This could be even more harmful if their diets lack zinc to begin with.

· Kelp contains iodine. Iodine excess causes alterations in thyroid activity. Know how much iodine is in your chosen brand of kelp before deciding how much to use in the diet.

· Diets in this book are based on NRC recommendations.

· Insufficient or excessive amounts of nutrients may affect genetic expression and cause problems that may be incorrectly viewed as genetic flaws.

---

8   Castillo, V. A., Rodriguez, M. S., Lalia, J. C., Pisarev, M. A. (2003) Morphologic Changes in the Thyroid Glands of Puppies Fed a High-Iodine Commercial Diet. *The International Journal of Applied Research in Veterinary Medicine*; 1 (1).

CHAPTER 4
The Girl

WE MUST CONSIDER MANY FACTORS BEFORE BREEDING a dog, including health, temperament, pedigree, age, titles, and, of course, timing. Sometimes we breed only for beautiful conformation. A dog may have a perfect head, wonderful gait and stunning coat, but what about health? Health must come first if we are to have any hope of producing healthy dogs. There is no point in breeding for any other reason. Health must be our primary focus or we risk producing dogs as fragile as sandcastles: lovely to look at but destroyed by the slightest gust of wind. Any experienced long-time breeder knows that looks can be improved much more quickly than health.

An ideal breeding scenario would involve healthy dogs with at least two generations of healthy predecessors. Reality can be quite different. We cannot always find ideal dogs, and sometimes problems arise in our own kennels despite our best efforts. Nutrition is a good place to start to address these problems.

Your female puppy should be considered a mother-in-waiting. Her body will be called upon to become pregnant, carry all puppies to term successfully, whelp naturally and feed the puppies with nutrient-rich milk. Feed her for these upcoming events now. Do not wait until she is about to be bred to start thinking about the nutrients she requires. She must be able to support her puppies both as they grow inside her and after they are whelped while remaining healthy herself. She will not be able to do this successfully and without compromising her own health if she does not have the nutrient reserves she needs. Those reserves can only be available if her diet is correct from the start.

Ally

Ally is the first dog in her particular kennel to be raised on an entirely home-prepared diet. She is 12 weeks old, weighs 15 pounds and eats the following cooked diet daily:

Ally's Daily Cooked Diet

1 egg, hard boiled

5 ounces beef heart, simmered

⅛ ounce beef liver, braised

2 ounces ground turkey

6 ounces potato, boiled with skin

2 ounces zucchini, raw

⅐ canned oyster

⅛ teaspoon table salt

1/16 teaspoon kelp

2 ¼ teaspoons di-calcium phosphate[9]

1 teaspoon safflower oil

500 milligrams wild salmon oil

50 IU vitamin E

2 capsules, Allergy Research MultiMin™[10]

1 capsule, cod liver oil[11]

This cooked diet provides 754 kilocalories that break down as 40% from protein, 22% from carbohydrates and 38 from fat.

Rather than having to cut one oyster into seven pieces, Ally is fed one oyster per week. Raw oysters should never be fed, as they can carry an organism (fluke) that is deadly to dogs.

This diet meets Ally's nutrient requirements for now, but it will need to be changed as she grows. Feeding enough of this same diet to meet her caloric requirement may not meet Ally's growing need for higher amounts of vitamins and minerals. However, feeding yet more food is not an option either. When a dog consumes too many kilocalories, weight

---

9   The di-calcium phosphate used here provides 1,025 milligrams of calcium and 900 milligrams of phosphorus per teaspoon.

10 Allergy Research MultiMin™ is a brand name for a mineral supplement made by Allergy Research/ Nutricology. It is available in some stores and online.

11 The cod liver oil capsule in this diet plan provides 1,250 IU of vitamin A and 100 IU of vitamin D.

gain can be expected regardless of the actual volume of food. In the case of growing puppies, excess weight on a skeleton that is not yet ready to support it can be the cause of many skeletal problems.

Potential Havoc

All puppies require a good diet, but a mother-to-be has special concerns. Her body needs to handle conception, pregnancy, whelping and lactation. Ally cannot perform these functions without compromising her own health unless both her puppy and adult diets provide the required amount of all the vitamins and minerals at each life stage.

The following tables show some of the major roles that specific nutrients play in the body as well as some of the possible results of deficiency and excess.

Vitamin Functions; Signs of Deficiencies & Excesses

VITAMINS	FUNCTION	SIGNS OF DEFICIENCY	SIGNS OF EXCESS
Vitamin A	Immune system function, fetal development, prevents night blindness, aids in formation of bones, antioxidant	Reproductive failure, tearing, night blindness, poor coat, weakness of hind legs	Weight loss, anorexia, bone decalcification
Vitamin B1 (thiamine)	Brain function, digestion, energy, appetite, carbohydrate metabolism	Cardiac disorders, weight loss, abnormal reflexes, dehydration, convulsions	No toxicity recorded
Vitamin B2 (riboflavin)	Enzyme functions, metabolism of fats, proteins, carbohydrates, healthy skin	Reduced fertility, dry and scaly skin, muscle weakness, anemia	No toxicity recorded
Vitamin B3 (niacinamide)	Enzyme functions, healthy skin, function of nervous system	Ulceration of mucus membranes, bloody diarrhea	Inflammation, irritation and itchiness of skin
Vitamin B5 (pantothenic acid)	Energy metabolism, fat, protein and carbohydrate metabolism	Gastritis, fatty liver, rapid breathing and heart rate, convulsions	No toxicity recorded

Vitamin Functions; Signs of Deficiencies & Excesses (continued)

VITAMINS	FUNCTION	SIGNS OF DEFICIENCY	SIGNS OF EXCESS
Vitamin B6 (pyridoxine)	Hormone regulation, taurine and carnitine synthesis, activation of genes, immune response, glucose generation	Weight loss in puppies, high serum iron level	Muscle weakness, convulsions
Vitamin B12 (cobalamin)	Cell formation, supports nerve structure, enzyme function	Anemia, loss of appetite, changes in bone marrow	No toxicity recorded
Biotin	Healthy skin, utilization of other B vitamins	Excessive hair loss, anorexia, diarrhea, scaly skin	No toxicity recorded
Choline	Neurotransmitter	Increased alkaline phosphatase, fatty liver	No toxicity recorded
Folic Acid	Amino acid metabolism, proper function of red blood cells	Decline in hemoglobin, malabsorption	No toxicity recorded
Vitamin C	Antioxidant, enhances iron absorption, tissue growth and repair	Increased susceptibility to disease	Gastritis, diarrhea
Vitamin D	Bone mineralization, muscle contraction, proper absorption of calcium and phosphorus	Softening of the bones, weakness, poor eruption of permanent teeth	Weight loss, calcification of soft tissue, diarrhea, dehydration
Vitamin E	Antioxidant, cell membrane integrity	Reproductive failure, retinal atrophy, impaired immunity	Anorexia
Vitamin K	Normal blood coagulation	Increased clotting time	No toxicity recorded

Mineral Functions; Signs of Deficiencies & Excesses

MINERALS	FUNCTION	SIGNS OF DEFICIENCY	SIGNS OF EXCESS
Calcium	Constituent of teeth and bones, muscle function, transmission of nerve impulses	Splayed toes, skeletal abnormalities, secondary, hyperparathyroidism	Skeletal abnormalities, zinc, copper, iron deficiencies
Phosphorus	Constituent of teeth and bones, energy production, DNA and RNA structure	Depraved appetite, swelling and bowing of limbs in puppies	Calcium deficiency
Potassium	Osmotic balance, muscle contraction, transmission of nerve impulses	Weakness, decreased muscle tone, paralysis	Does not occur unless there is a low volume of urine
Magnesium	Mineral structure of bones and teeth, enzyme functions, nerve cell and muscle membrane stability	Retarded growth, soft tissue calcification, spreading of toes	Diarrhea due to poor absorption
Iron	Production of hemoglobin, oxygenation of red blood cells, energy metabolism	Anemia, pale mucous membranes, weakness	Gastrointestinal and tissue damage
Zinc	Wound healing, protein synthesis, skin health, cell replication	Skin lesions, poor weight gain, generalized thinning of hair coat, decreased testicular development	Calcium and/or copper deficiency
Copper	Bone formation, pigmentation, immune function, iron metabolism, blood cell formation	Bone lesions, slow growth, hair depigmentation	Liver damage
Manganese	Neurological function, bone development, enzyme functions	Impaired reproduction, stiffness, abortion	Impaired fertility
Iodine	Normal function of thyroid gland	Enlargement of thyroid gland, weight gain or loss, dry, sparse coat	Same as deficiency, dandruff, excessive tearing
Sodium	Transmission of nerve impulses, regulation of osmotic balance	Weight loss, fatigue, high blood pressure, salt hunger	Increased heart rate and water intake

Before Breeding Ally

Alley is now two years old. She has just had a complete check-up by the veterinarian. Her breeder knows that both Ally and the male she has selected should be checked for infection. After all, Ally has never been bred before, but the male has been used at stud for some time. Since he has encountered many bitches, he is more likely to have an infection. Ally was not grossly overweight but needed to lose a couple of pounds. Her breeder made sure that healthy weight loss was achieved because she knows to never attempt weight loss during pregnancy. At her ideal weight, Ally now has a much better chance of conceiving, carrying her pups without difficulty, whelping easily and producing enough milk.

Her veterinarian has carefully checked for fleas, and a stool sample was inspected for parasites. This was an important step because fleas and worms can cause anemia, which could cause serious problems during Ally's pregnancy.

A bitch that shows a problem in her blood values is a poor candidate for breeding. She is more likely to have weak puppies and have trouble feeding them. Luckily, Ally's blood values show normal bone marrow, liver and kidney functions, and no sign of infection.

The Rendezvous

Too often, either the bitch or the male is uninterested in the other. Instinct can be a fairly good indicator of how a breeding will go. More often than not, Nature is trying to tell us something when we need to force a pair of dogs together.

The will to reproduce is a natural instinct, and dogs do not lack it. They will eagerly mount other dogs, furniture and human legs as proof that instinct is strong. Dogs also know when they are interested in another dog. They do not need humans to tell them so. A bitch in heat will mount just about anything that moves. When she is unwilling to mate with a male that has been selected for her, it might be better to listen to her. Hormones could be at fault. Instinctively not liking or fearing the other dog is enough to set off a hormonal reaction.

She is likely to conceive whether or not she accepts the male willingly, but the long-term health of the puppies may be in question if the pair is forced together. Perhaps this is because dogs have instincts that we may not fully understand and can tell when another dog is not completely healthy. Whatever the reason, my experience in working with breeders is that trusting the bitch and dog to mate naturally is what works best. After all, in a natural setting, the strongest animals choose each other without human beings coercing — or even forcing — them together.

Chapter Summary

- The female puppy is a mother-in-waiting.
- Diet should be excellent from the time a dog is weaned.
- A veterinary visit prior to breeding will let you know about a dog's general health and can help prevent many common problems seen during pregnancy and whelping.
- The male is more likely to have an infection than the female.
- The bitch should be at her ideal weight before being bred.
- Never put a pregnant bitch on a weight-loss diet.
- When two dogs refuse to mate with each other, it may be better not to force the situation.

CHAPTER 5
Ally's Pregnancy

M OST BREEDERS I WORK WITH HAVE CONCERNS about feeding bitches properly during gestation. Their greatest worries are generally how to deal with a bitch that has lost interest in her food and how much calcium should be added to the diet.

Ally's breeder has heard that excess vitamin A can cause cleft palates and wants to know more about this. She is also considering starting Ally on a raw diet. Should she?

Do Not Panic

Experienced breeders know that it is not uncommon for a bitch to lose her appetite during the second to fourth week of pregnancy. Think of it as morning sickness. This is due to hormonal changes that can cause nausea and changes in appetite. Some bitches will eagerly eat foods with little nutrition and refuse what the breeder thinks is healthy. This is not a cause for worry either. If a bitch has been fed a good diet before her pregnancy, her body has stores of vitamins and minerals to draw upon.

Foods that are not typically in her regular diet are fine to try, and some of the foods she may crave are not as unhealthy as we think. For instance, one slice of buttered whole-wheat toast, while not providing nearly enough of each nutrient, still provides some B vitamins and small amounts of all minerals. About three quarters of a teaspoon of butter provides 36 calories, some vitamin A and some essential fatty acids. Even if she refuses almost all foods, she will be fine as long as she is healthy during this period.

A Special Time

While pregnancy is a special time of life for all animals, it may surprise you to know that there are few necessary dietary changes. For example, calcium does not need to be added to a diet that was balanced to begin with. As her appetite grows and the bitch consumes more food, she will automatically ingest the extra calcium she needs. However, it is very important not to overfeed. She may want more food than she needs during the last half of her pregnancy. That is fine as long as she does not become overweight, because an overweight bitch will have more trouble whelping. The ideal time to increase food rations is between weeks four and five. This will give her the extra nutrients that she needs.

Calcium

If the bitch's diet before pregnancy met her nutritional needs, adding extra calcium during pregnancy can backfire. She does need more calcium, but as mentioned above, simply consuming more of her regular diet will provide it. Adding more calcium can result in excessive levels and suppress parathyroid hormone production. This in turn interferes with normal calcium metabolism and storage. Ironically, too much calcium has the opposite of the desired effect; as the body is now unable to metabolize stored calcium, the bitch is at higher risk for eclampsia, a dangerous and even fatal condition in pregnant or nursing bitches.

My anecdotal evidence seems to support these scientific findings. Many of the raw-fed pregnant bitches I have worked with have their own calcium schedule in mind. Clients that have fed a bitch plenty of raw meaty bones (RMBs) in the past find that she is likely to bury them by the time she is six to seven weeks pregnant.

Bitches on a balanced raw diet do very well. If the diet is changed to provide only meat, which can satisfy roughly 10% of calcium requirement at best, the bitch will draw on her own mineral stores. This decreases bone density and puts her at risk for skeletal problems and loss of teeth.

Carbohydrates

When working with breeders, I always add carbohydrates to the diet of a pregnant bitch. An early study[12] indicated that live births were only 63% and mortality rates after birth were high when higher levels of

---

12 Romsos, D. R., Palmer, H. J., Muiruri, K. L., Bennink, M. R. (Apr 1981) Influence of a low carbohydrate diet on performance of pregnant and lactating dogs. *The Journal of Nutrition*; 111 (4): 678-89.

carbohydrates were not included in the diet. However, further studies indicated that bitches did not need a source of carbohydrate during pregnancy and lactation as long as dietary protein was increased from 26% (the amount in the first study) to 45% or 51% (the amounts in two other studies).[13] So why continue to add carbohydrates to the diet?

In my experience, not all bitches tolerate a diet with 45% protein. Some experience diarrhea as the pregnancy progresses. Fat is another consideration. Most meat sources provide a good deal of fat even if the meat looks lean. Increased amounts of fat can also be the underlying cause of diarrhea. I choose not to risk a high-fat diet. I always add a little rice or potato to a pregnant bitch's diet. I have found that adding carbohydrates often results in better milk production. Carbohydrates also provide a source of energy, which allows protein in the diet be used for building puppy tissues, increasing protein in the milk, and maintaining the bitch's lean body mass. In my opinion, it is better to add carbohydrates than risk unhealthy pups and low milk production.

Vitamin A and Cleft Palate

A 1967 study showed that 125,000 IU of vitamin A per kilogram of body weight during days 17 – 22 of gestation produced cleft palates in newborn pups.[14] It would be difficult, if not impossible, to provide this much vitamin A in a home-prepared diet, even if we fed one pound of beef liver and one tablespoon of cod liver oil per day to a 40-pound dog. The study provided over 1,000 times the recommended amount of vitamin A. However, since it is not known if cleft palates can be caused by a lesser amount of vitamin A than in this study, I choose to err on the side of caution.

The available brands of cod liver oil provide varying amounts of vitamins A and D. Both of these vitamins are critical to bone forma-tion as well as skin health and normal vision. Cod liver oil also provides omega-3 fatty acids. Beef liver contains a high level of vitamin A and is an excellent source of copper. Ally can consume both cod liver oil and beef liver during her pregnancy, but it is very important not to exceed her needs, which should be based on her body weight before pregnancy. She does not require any more or less vitamin A when she is pregnant.

13 Blaza, S. E., Booles, D. B., Burger, I.H. (1989) Is carbohydrate essential for pregnancy and lactation in dogs? *Waltham Symposium No 7; Nutrition of the Dog and Cat;* Chapter 12: 229-242.
14 Wiersig, D. O. , Swenson, M.J. (1967) Teratogenicity of vitamin A in the canine. *Federation Proceedings;* 26: 486.

When increasing Ally's food intake during her pregnancy, the breeder should restrict animal products that provide vitamin A. While the volume of other foods can increase, those that provide vitamin A are better left at the original amounts.

Changing the Diet

Ally's breeder is tempted to switch to a raw diet. However, it is better to do this after the puppies have gone to their new homes and Ally's lifestyle is back to normal. At the moment, the stress of pregnancy and Ally's nausea make this a bad time for dietary changes. The fact that Ally may have food sensitivities or allergies that have not yet been discovered could complicate the situation even more.

Like all animals, Ally may have become a subclinical carrier of disease. When the immune system fights unfriendly organisms, one of three outcomes takes place: the body wins and we never know that a battle even took place, the body manages to overcome the organism but later succumbs again from stress or concurrent disease, or the body loses the battle altogether. Pregnancy brings a certain amount of stress to the body. Ally has never consumed raw foods before, which makes her more likely to initially fall victim to unfriendly bacteria if she switches now. In addition, if she is also carrying an infection during this time, her body is set up for failure. The best approach is to ensure that her current diet is excellent and try another feeding method later.

Also keep in mind that any quick dietary changes can upset the stomach. The breeder needs time to understand any reaction to a new diet. If Ally were to vomit raw meat, it would be unclear whether the food itself, the introduction of a new food, or simply nausea due to pregnancy is the cause.

Chapter Summary

- Most bitches will lose their appetites and/or become fussy eaters during weeks 2 – 4 of pregnancy.
- Do not overfeed as this risks obesity and difficult labor.
- There is no need to increase the amount of calcium in a pregnant bitch's diet if the original diet provided enough.
- Too much calcium can lead to eclampsia.
- The diet should include either carbohydrates or high levels of protein. If in doubt, do not hesitate to include carbohydrates.
- The vitamin A content of the diet should be based on the normal, healthy weight of a bitch before pregnancy.
- Switching from one feeding method to another is best done before a bitch becomes pregnant or after her puppies have been weaned.

CHAPTER 6
The Puppies Have Arrived

ALLY WHELPED HER PUPPIES like a professional. She ate the placentas, and the pups were nursing in no time. The breeder is very pleased about this because the colostrum in first milk is very important to the newborns; it allows Ally to pass on some of her own immunity to diseases.

Gut Closure

"Closure" refers to changes in the intestinal tract that prevent further absorption of immunoglobulins and other large intact proteins.

Claudia Kirk, DVM, PhD, DACVIM, DACVN, of the University of Tennessee, showed that puppies begin gut closure to large molecules like those in colostrum by 16 hours after birth. Complete closure occurs in 72 hours maximum. Newborns are very vulnerable during this time because their immature immune systems are unable to fight bacteria and other dangerous foreign bodies. Since the gut is permeable, immunoglobulins in the bitch's colostrum are absorbed intact to ensure protection. If the gut were to remain open, foreign invaders would also be able to get into the body and cause serious illness or death.

Lactation

The dietary requirements of a nursing bitch are based on litter size, stage of lactation and previous nutritional history. In most cases, feeding her one and one half times the regular amount of food during the first week, twice the amount the second week, and up to three to five times the third week works very well. However, the quality of her original diet must also be considered.

There are changes in the composition of a bitch's milk throughout lactation. A study from U.C. Davis[15] shows that "protein concentration is high in samples collected on day 1 (143 g/L), decreased through day 21 (68.4 g/L), and increased thereafter. Iron, zinc, copper, and magnesium concentrations decreased during lactation, whereas calcium and phosphorus concentrations increased. Calcium-to-phosphorus ratio remained constant throughout lactation (approximately 1.6:1)."

Clearly, the lactating bitch needs a high quality diet if we expect her to produce enough milk.

Mom's First Meal

Some bitches are voraciously hungry after whelping their puppies. Others are too exhausted and busy with their little ones to show any interest in food. Every breeder seems to have a favorite food offering for the first meal after whelping. Here is an easy recipe that has worked well for me for many years:

Post-Whelping Meal

1 ounce dry oats, cooked
2 whole eggs
3 ounces whole milk yogurt
½ eggshell

Be sure that the bitch already tolerates these foods. This is a poor time to be introducing new foods only to discover that they cause her to have diarrhea. I recommend that bitches be introduced to this mixture before their whelp date. If she tolerates it at that time, she should tolerate it later as well.

Calcium plays a critical role during lactation. A bitch that does not want to eat should be allowed to eat anything she likes that provides calcium. Vanilla ice cream, goat's milk and/or whole milk ricotta cheese (note that this is much better than cottage cheese because the calcium to phosphorus ratio is 1.3:1) can often tempt a bitch to eat. However, do not

15 Adkins, Y., Lepine, A. J., Lönnerdal, B. (Aug 2001) Changes in protein and nutrient composition of milk throughout lactation in dogs. *American Journal of Veterinary Research*; 62(8): 1266-1272.

supplement too heavily with calcium right after the bitch has whelped, because her body needs to adjust to releasing calcium. She is not lactating heavily so calcium is not as critical as it becomes later on.

By the third week of lactation, heavy lactation places a dramatic burden on a bitch's calcium reserves, and sometimes her body is unable to compensate for the loss. When this occurs, eclampsia may result. Eclampsia is a condition in which the blood calcium level drops, causing the bitch to become nervous, tremble, and have muscle spasms that increase body temperature. This fever does not cause the seizures, but high fever can lead to death.

Milk Replacer

Ally has plenty of milk for her puppies; however not all bitches do. Some have plenty of milk but refuse to nurse their puppies. Being prepared for this problem can saves lives.

Replacing mother's milk is serious business. No formula can replicate natural milk perfectly; however, sometimes there is no choice. When a bitch has no milk or refuses to feed her pups, or if the puppies are orphans, we can choose to either buy a high quality formula like Esbilac® or make our own. I prefer Esbilac® because it is convenient, consistent, and provides proper nutrition at a very critical stage of life.

There are a number of home-prepared formulas on the Internet and in books. While it is better to be prepared with some Esbilac®, in a pinch (and only for a very short period of time), the following can be helpful:

Puppy Formula

1 cup milk
1 cup cream
⅔ cup boiled water
1 ¼ teaspoons bone meal powder
6 drops of corn syrup

Preparation: When the mixture is at body temperature, add 6 drops of a children's liquid multivitamin and a pinch of acidophilus (a probiotic).

I have found that some newborn pups cannot tolerate egg yolk right away. Sometimes this is because their immature livers and low bile acid production cannot clear the cholesterol and fat out of the digestive tract. However, if the above formula is to be used for more than 24 hours, the addition of 3 – 4 egg yolks becomes necessary in order to add more kilocalories without adding a lot more bulk to the food. If the puppies cannot tolerate egg, protein powder (4 teaspoons) and oil (I usually start by adding 1 teaspoon of safflower oil) can substitute.

The First Few Weeks – Vitamin C

For the next short while, the puppies are eating, sleeping and keeping their mother busy cleaning up after them. Ally's breeder keeps her clean, although Ally seems a little on edge and would prefer to be left alone. This behavioral change is not unique to Ally. The emotional and physical stress on a bitch at this time is, understandably, sometimes more than she can bear. Hormone changes also add to mood and behavioral changes.

There is no physiological basis for the addition of vitamin C during this stage, and no studies I have found to support the addition of this vitamin at this time. Breeders often report positive results supplementing with Ester-C® to help their bitch calm down. The dosage depends on bowel tolerance because excess vitamin C can cause loose stool. Generally, I suggest 250 milligrams of Ester-C® per day for a bitch weighing 40 – 50 pounds. Supplementation earlier than two weeks after parturition seems to have no effect, but may be helpful after week two. Ester-C® is much gentler to the stomach and this is reason enough to choose it over other forms of vitamin C.

Before deciding to add vitamin C in any form, remember that it is excreted in urine. When it combines with calcium excreted through urine, there is a chance that calcium oxalate crystals will form. Never give vitamin C to a dog that has a history of calcium oxalate crystals in urine.

Weaning

Once the puppies are about four weeks old, Mom's milk alone no longer supports their nutrient requirements. This is when most breeders begin to soak some dry food or offer a little canned food to puppies. Ally's breeder wants to offer a home-prepared, cooked diet. Her friend has a litter of puppies that she wants to wean to a home-prepared raw diet.

Puppies have higher demand for vitamins and minerals than adult dogs. The adult body can be likened to a finished house undergoing constant renovation, whereas the youngster's body is a house being built. Do a poor job building the house and it is easily flattened by the slightest gust of wind.

To provide the large amounts of nutrients that a pup requires without adding an excess volume of food that the puppy will not or cannot consume, we need to feed very nutrient-dense foods. However, even this approach can backfire. The key is in knowing the caloric limit. This is exactly the same scenario as we discussed in the chapter about feeding Noah. However, puppies are even more difficult because they require more of each nutrient while being able to eat less volume.

A dog that will weigh thirty pounds as an adult will require about 350 kilocalories per day when it weighs four pounds at the age of about four weeks. The *nutrient* requirements of this puppy will double when he weighs eight pounds but his caloric requirements will only be about 650 calories. Obviously, we cannot feed twice the amount of the original diet without the pup becoming overweight. Yet, we need twice the amounts of nutrients. When the pup is six months old and weighs about twenty pounds, he will need about 790 calories per day. He now weighs fives times what he did at four weeks of age, but if we were to feed five times the amount of food (even if he were able to consume this amount), we would have an obese pup. Clearly, the growth and nutrient requirement curves are not parallel.

My puppy diets are geared toward the individual. There is no rule of thumb to follow because food tolerances can vary just as individual weight, conformation, activity level and caloric needs do. When working with pups, I change the diet as the dog grows so that nutrient requirements, based on body weight, are met within caloric boundaries. However, there are some guideposts along the way that may be helpful.

Weaning to a cooked or raw diet should be done in stages. Puppies tend toward sloppy stool when their digestive systems are challenged with new foods. I prefer to feed as many parts of a single whole animal as possible. Some examples are, beef heart, beef liver, beef chunk meat and bone meal or turkey necks, turkey gizzard and turkey heart. My reasoning is that if a pup is going to develop a food allergy or intolerance, life will be easier for breeder, puppy, and pet owner alike if the reaction is to a single meat source. Also, a whole animal provides a much better nutrient profile than meals "diluted" with other foods.

Food Allergies and Oral Tolerance

There is some question about exposing young animals to a variety of food sources. The ability of any animal's body to ignore foreign matter is called oral tolerance. As the puppy's immune system matures, it learns what proteins are tolerable and which proteins require attack. The mature gut has a protective mucosal barrier that is only one cell thick and not always a perfect barrier, so proteins from the food can sometimes slip through. The gut's immune system ignores the proteins it learned to tolerate and reacts, sometimes very aggressively, to destroy the other foreign proteins with antibodies, white blood cells and inflammatory chemicals like histamine.

Food allergy is an example of this aggressive response and when allergies develop against previously tolerated proteins, oral tolerance is lost. When this occurs, the general recommendation is to change the dog's diet to a recipe that contains only a single meat source, one that the dog has not shown an allergic reaction to. Since natural allergic responses in dogs can be closely related to that in humans[16] weaning allergy prone pups onto a single meat source diet may promote better health by reducing the chances of an allergic reaction at an early age.

Carbohydrates

Obviously, if feeding commercial diets during the weaning process, carbohydrates will be included in the food. There is some debate about this issue in the home-prepared diet circle. When do puppies become able to digest carbohydrates in the first place? How do digestive enzymes change before and after weaning?

In searching for answers, I contacted Dr. Randal Buddington, Professor of Biology at University of California, Davis. Dr. Buddington states "The ability of very young dogs up to 3 weeks of age to digest complex diets is going to be very limited. Puppies begin developing the enzymes needed to digest more complex food between 3 and 5 weeks of age. The enzymes needed to digest protein tend to go up a little bit earlier because they do need to digest the casein and other proteins present in milk. Diets at the time of weaning should be composed of highly digestible proteins from animal tissues. Most veterinarians and breeders would recognize that you don't want to put a young puppy on something made mostly out

---

16 Buchanan, B. B., Frick, O. L. (May 2002) The dog as a model for food allergy. *Annals of the New York Academy of Sciences; 964:* 173-83.

of corn or soy — you want a high quality diet to get him going well. We have not yet determined what causes dogs to begin producing the enzymes needed to digest carbohydrates because those enzymes only increase after the dogs begin eating food with carbohydrates in it, at about 4 weeks of age. As a result, we don't know whether the increase was genetically programmed or if it was in response to having some starch from diet in the intestine."[17]

This information tells us that weaning too early can backfire. Further, the addition of carbohydrates to the diet of a young puppy should wait until this dog is at least four weeks old.

Lactose Intolerance

Lactose is a milk sugar. Lactase is an enzyme that helps to break down lactose. When growing animals are weaned off of milk, they stop making as much of this enzyme. The result is an inability to digest lactose properly. This becomes evident to the dog owner when the dog has diarrhea and/or vomits after eating foods that contain lactose. If lactose-containing foods are fed throughout life, the gut continues to produce lactase. "Use it or lose it" applies here too.

Weaning Off Mom's Milk

Some breeders take the puppies away from the bitch's milk earlier than I would like to see. There is no reason to do this unless the bitch is refusing the puppies or her health demands that the youngsters not be fed by her for an extended period of time. Most bitches make excellent mothers and will continue to offer themselves to their pups. Her instinct is one of the most important keys to the weaning process. Not only does she know when her puppies need nourishment but she has a sixth sense about which one needs more encouragement for a while longer. The soothing comfort of Mom's milk and warmth is part of the social bonding and cues an increased response to being touched. Mom does not give it to pups that do not require it. The bitch will make it very clear to her pups when it is time to leave her alone. Until she makes this obvious, early weaning away from her milk can do more harm than good. Not only might a pup need the extra calories and nutrition that the bitch offers, but Mom tends to nurse weaker pups a little longer. They may be weaker physically or emotionally but no matter what her reasons, Mom usually knows best.

---

17 Buddington, R. K. (March 2005) Private correspondence.

The pups are now eating more whole food and Mom is putting less energy into milk production. This is the time to start trimming back her calories. Of course, we want the bitch to return to her well-conditioned self. Hormonal changes and the labor-intensive job of raising her pups usually translates to a raggedy coat. If she is a long-eared dog with patience for her playful babies, her ears have probably been chewed as well. While this does not seem to bother her, the breeder heading for the show ring cringes just about now.

Getting Ally Back Into Shape

Since Ally's energy needs are not as high as they were when she was pregnant or lactating, she is now consuming the same number of calories as she did prior to having puppies. All nutrients, being provided in healthy amounts, will help her to regain her figure and grow a nice coat again. In the meantime, brushing her daily will help to loosen any coat that is about to shed as well as removing some dry skin. In addition, brushing Ally will increase circulation to the skin, bringing along nutrients for hair growth and repair. Ally's diet is rich in eggs for their high quality protein, some lean fish such as canned mackerel for added protein and the omega-3 fatty acids, red meats for their B vitamins, iron, copper and zinc, and fresh fruits and vegetables.

Some bitches respond very well to the addition of grains at this time. Grains add soluble fiber that gut microbes use, producing short-chain fatty acids that contribute to the health of the gut lining and so, to Mom's health. Grains are a good source of carbohydrates that have a protein-sparing effect. It may be for this reason that I continue to see new mothers growing coat faster when grains are added to their diets.

Ally is being exercised regularly. She is still not keen to leave her pups for too long but by the time they are seven weeks old, she manages two half-hour walks per day and her muscle tone is evident.

Chapter Summary

- The changes in the intestinal tract of a puppy start at 16 hours after birth.

- Feeding a bitch one and one half times the regular amount of food during the first week of lactation, twice the amount the second week and up to three times the third week works very well. Some bitches require as much as five times their maintenance energy during peak lactation.

- Esbilac® is an excellent milk replacer.

- Supplementation with Vitamin C, 2 weeks after parturition may help the irritability of the new mother.

- Feed a puppy as many parts of a whole animal as possible rather than choosing many sources of protein.

- Do not introduce carbohydrates until a puppy is at least 4 weeks old, preferably later.

- The great majority of bitches will continue to nurse their puppies for a longer period of time than many people allow. Following the lead of the new mother usually bodes well for the emotional and physical health of the puppy.

- A high quality diet, sometimes with the addition of grains, will help the bitch regain her normal coat faster. Carbohydrates provide energy while sparing protein so that the body can use that protein for hair, skin and enzymes, helping Mom to return to pre-pregnancy physique and health.

CHAPTER 7
Puppies in Forever Homes

A LLY'S PUPS ARE IN THEIR PERMANENT HOMES. Each has a wonderful owner who is very willing to feed a home-prepared diet. Three of the puppies (Beamer, Jackson and Alexa) are going to be fed a raw diet, while the other two (Travis and Zach) will be fed cooked foods.

The breeder tried her best to match the personality of each puppy to the lifestyle of the owner. Jackson is a laid back, easy-going puppy who will fit in nicely with his couch-potato people. Travis is with another breeder, waiting to become the star of the show ring. Beamer is always on the go and the perfect match for his owners, who are involved in agility trials. Alexa will make a wonderful companion for the seven-year old boy in her new family. Zach will be multi-tasking as the companion of three adults, two with a passion for hunting and another who enjoys down time in front of the television.

We are going to watch five different puppies, each with unique metabolisms as well as lifestyles, grow up. Clearly, one diet will not be appropriate for all of them. The following sections will look at the differences in their diets.

Beamer – On the Go
Like his siblings, Beamer is expected to weigh forty pounds as an adult dog. At eight weeks of age, he weighs ten pounds. His needs are currently met by eating the following daily diet along with four supplements given per week rather than per day.

Beamer's Daily Raw Diet

9 ounces beef heart
4 ounces ground beef, lean, 15% fat
1 ½ ounces turkey neck
¼ ounce beef liver
7 ounces sweet potato
4 capsules, cod liver oil per week
4 capsules, Allergy Research MultiMin™ per week
1 capsule, vitamin E 100 IU per week
3 capsules, wild salmon oil per week
¹⁄₁₆ teaspoon kelp
1 ¼ teaspoons bone meal
4 milligrams zinc citrate or gluconate

This raw diet provides 780 kilocalories that break down as 40% from protein, 24% from carbohydrates and 36% from fat.

Notice that Beamer's diet is slightly more varied than what we would have chosen during weaning at the breeder. Foods are limited to turkey, beef and sweet potato to better meet nutrient requirements.

Rather than cutting one ounce of beef liver into fourths, so Beamer can eat ¼ ounce of liver daily, it would be acceptable to simply give him one ounce every four days or half an ounce every other day.

Multivitamin and multi-mineral supplements do not taste good. Opening a capsule and giving Beamer half capsule daily is likely to turn him off his meals and might upset his stomach. However, one capsule inside a hand held piece of food every other day can work well.

Jackson – The Couch Potato

Could we feed Beamer's diet to Jackson? Not without Jackson gaining a lot of weight at an age when he should be kept on the slim side. Jackson is not nearly as energetic as his brother, and that translates to needing fewer kilocalories. As we have discussed, simply feeding less food means supplying fewer amounts of nutrients. While Jackson may not require the same number of kilocalories, his protein, fat, vitamin and mineral requirements are exactly the same as his brother's.

Jackson's Daily Raw Diet

5 ounces sweet potato
10 ounces lamb heart
2 ounces ground lamb
1 ounce ground turkey
¼ ounce beef liver
1 ½ teaspoons di-calcium phosphate
½ teaspoon NOW® Calcium Carbonate Powder
1 capsule, cod liver oil
¹⁄₁₆ teaspoon kelp
1 capsule, vitamin E 100 IU per week
7 milligrams zinc citrate or gluconate
250 milligrams wild salmon oil
4 capsules, Allergy Research MultiMin™ per week

This raw diet provides 713 kilocalories that break down as 37% from protein, 20% from carbohydrates and 43% from fat.

Alexa – Trouble In Paradise

Alexa came bouncing into her new home with all the enthusiasm we might expect of a happy puppy. Her owner is friendly with Beamer's owner and they decided to feed the same diet because buying foods in bulk would save money. Alexa developed diarrhea almost instantly, her energy level dropped and it was suspected that the pup was reacting to beef. Was she?

A veterinarian diagnosed Alexa with giardia. A round of medication got things under control; however, like many dogs, Alexa may have some gastrointestinal trouble and food sensitivities. A new diet of boiled chicken and rice agreed with the pup, so her owner now prefers to feed a diet based on raw chicken with cooked rice. A bit of beef liver is also added to provide copper (the diet would be grossly deficient in copper otherwise as chicken liver is a poor source of copper).

Alexa's Daily Raw Diet

2 ounces chicken, dark meat with skin, without bone
1 ounce chicken carcass
7 chicken gizzards
2 ounces white rice (raw weight)
½ ounce beef liver
¹⁄₁₆ teaspoon No-Salt®
¹⁄₁₆ teaspoon kelp
6¼ milligrams vitamin B compound (1/8 of a 50 milligrams tablet)
1½ teaspoons di-calcium phosphate
250 milligrams wild salmon oil
9 capsules, Allergy Research MultiMin™ (per week)
5 capsules, cod liver oil (per week)
1 capsule, vitamin E 100 IU (per week)

This raw diet provides 730 kilocalories that break down as 39 % from protein, 27 % from carbohydrates and 34% from fat.

Notice that the diet calls for white, rather than brown rice, which provides much more fiber. Some dogs digest brown rice quite well, but the husks, being indigestible fiber, are visible in the stool. Since Alexa has just been though some tummy trouble, white rice is more agreeable.

Grains need to be well boiled. Once cup of rice to three cups of water is generally a good ratio but to make sure, perform a "pinch test." Once the rice seems to be cooked thoroughly, a grain held between thumb and forefinger should be easily flattened with very little pressure.

Can cooked and raw foods be combined? Absolutely. I have never worked with a client who experienced any problems. After all, dogs are scavengers. A healthy dog is an eager mouth on four legs. They can and do eat just about anything in any combination — cooked and raw — and generally do not experience problems.

Travis – The Show Dog

Travis is headed for the show ring and will be expected to perform as a stud dog once he has matured. His needs do not differ from those of a pet dog but we cannot afford to make any mistakes that would jeopardize his ability to perform at stud. Travis' muscle condition, cardiovascular health, body fat/weight, bone and joint health and ability to produce sperm must all be considerations. In addition to genetics and disease, these are influenced by diet.

His new home includes other dogs, so Travis is burning up some calories as he chases and plays between naps.

Travis' Daily Cooked Diet

2½ ounces beef heart, simmered

5½ ounces ground beef, lean, cooked

9 ounces potato with skin, cooked

1 ounce zucchini, steamed

½ ounce broccoli, steamed

3½ teaspoons bone meal

2 milligrams manganese

1 capsule, cod liver oil

¹⁄₁₆ teaspoon kelp

¼ vitamin B compound

2 capsules vitamin E, 100 IU per week

250 milligrams wild salmon oil

1,000 milligrams primrose oil

This cooked diet provides 767 kilocalories that break down as 39% from protein, 28% from carbohydrates and 33% from fat. *Note to the reader:* All weights are the yield of a food after it has been cooked.

Although dogs manufacture their own vitamin C, this vitamin can be helpful during times of stress. Like his siblings, Travis is in a new home; however he is also adjusting to other dogs. The addition of just a few grains of Ester-C® may help.

Keep in mind that there is threshold for bowel tolerance to any form of vitamin C. Give too much and the end result will be sloppy stool or even diarrhea. Puppies tend to have sensitive gastrointestinal tracts, so the best way of seeing how much a pup can tolerate is to increase the amount slowly. Keep track of how much is added to the food and cut back if a stool problem develops.

"This is Too Time Consuming"

Within a few days, Travis' owner feels overwhelmed by having to cook daily for her puppy. She will find that there is no need to cook each food separately. It will become much easier to simply make one or more week's worth of food and freeze it in daily servings for future use.

Chopping the potatoes and boiling them in the same pot with the beef heart and ground beef, flavors the potatoes and uses only one pot. Baking these foods would also work well. The zucchini and broccoli could be added to the pot 5 – 10 minutes before the other foods are cooked. Now, it is just a matter of removing the vegetables and mashing them into a pulp, combing them with the meats, adding the bone meal and kelp, and freezing the mixture in daily portions. The other supplements should be added to the food just prior to serving because they may lose potency or change the taste of food.

Manganese is a mineral that is usually available in the strength of 10 milligrams Travis only needs 2 milligrams per day, so his owner will simply give him one tablet every five days.

Zach – The Multi-tasker

Zach's family lives near a sheep farm where they are able to buy organic lamb meats at bargain prices. Zach seems to have a keen nose and moderate energy so he is likely to be great fun during trips to the field. We must make sure that he does not become pudgy, forcing his unprepared skeleton to support too much weight.

Zach's Daily Cooked Diet

5 ounces lamb heart, cooked

4 ounces ground lamb, cooked

1 ½ ounces brown rice, raw

1 ounce zucchini, steamed

1 ounce acorn squash, cooked

3 ¼ teaspoons bone meal

¼ capsule, Allergy Research MultiMin™

¹⁄₁₆ teaspoon kelp

¹⁄₁₆ teaspoon salt

¼ teaspoon No-Salt®

250 milligrams wild salmon oil
1 capsule, cod liver oil
2 capsules vitamin E, 100 IU per week

This cooked diet provides 768 kilocalories that break down as 36% from protein, 22% from carbohydrates and 42% from fat. *Note to the reader:* Other than the rice, which is noted as raw weight, all weights are the yield of a food after it has been cooked.

The first time this meal is prepared, Zach's owner will weigh the foods when raw and again after they have been cooked to ascertain how much weight is lost through cooking. There is then no further need to weigh each food every time a meal is prepared. Raw brown rice is boiled in a ratio of 1 cup rice to 4 – 4½ cups of water. While this is cooking, the meats can be placed in one pot or roasting pan and cooked as desired. The vegetables can be added either raw or cooked; however, in both cases, they need to be finely ground or mashed in order to accommodate proper digestion. When everything has been combined and cooled, bone meal, No-Salt® and kelp are added. To make things easier, Zach's owner could prepare 1 – 2 weeks' worth of food ahead of time and simply feed the remaining supplements in hand-held treats or add them to the food bowl. The only supplement that must be fed in a hand-held treat is the multi-mineral because the taste may turn Zach away from his food bowl otherwise. Since opening a capsule of the multi-mineral will make the treat taste odd, he will be given one full capsule every fourth day.

Training Treats

Our five puppies are off to a good start. As with all pups, their training involves daily treats. Highly valued treats tend to come in the form of protein such as the ever-popular liver treats. These add calories and protein, but in many cases also add more minerals, such as copper, to the diet. Packaged treats are not much of a problem because many contain copper oxide, a poorly absorbed form of copper. But fresh liver with a more bioavailable form of the mineral can cause problems. Copper stored in the liver can reach toxic levels. However, simply using part of the daily food intake as treats can prevent this problem altogether. Some examples are below.

Reserve one ounce of beef heart in a diet that calls for 5 ounces and use it as training treats. To make this ounce last longer, simply dry it in the oven and break off tiny morsels to give as rewards. The entire amount of beef liver that a diet calls for can be used as treats.

Most dogs love potatoes and sweet potatoes as treats. Thinly sliced and flavored with a dash of meat broth, they bake into crisp, tasty chips. Use some of the potato or sweet potato from the original diet to make the chips so that you do not add calories to the daily diet.

Remember that training based totally on treats, often backfires. Food is very motivating for most dogs — sometimes too much so. We want our dogs growing up in good physical shape. Packing on the pounds is very easy to do, but getting rid of that weight, especially in a growing puppy, can be challenging. Use low-calorie foods if you find that you need more treats. Most dogs like green beans, baby carrots, small pieces of fresh fruits or banana chips. However, they are not likely to be the motivational treat required when training for recall. Reserve the highly prized meat treats for serious training. Attention, affection and increased playtime will show the puppy that s/he is appreciated without adding any unwanted body weight.

Chapter Summary

· One diet does not fit all. Puppies have unique metabolisms and energy levels and require different amounts of calories even though they may have the same nutrient requirements.

· Fat tolerance needs to be considered.

· Limit the number of different animal sources in the diet.

· There is a bowel tolerance to any form of vitamin C.

· Beef liver is a good source of copper. Chicken and pork livers are poor sources.

· Use part of the daily diet as food treats to avoid weight gain.

· Puppies can learn to appreciate praise and affection in place of constant food rewards.

CHAPTER 8
Nutrients in Raw, Meaty Bones

A NALYSES OF RAW MEATY BONES, such as chicken necks, chicken wings, chicken backs, turkey necks and whole rabbit (without the head) can be found in my previous book. My goal for this book is to take things one step further by looking at some nutrient values of other raw meaty bones that many of my clients like to feed.

Note that in order to obtain a more accurate picture, samples were gathered from a variety of stores over the course of a few weeks. This reflects the way most of us shop. We may purchase some foods today, more next week or perhaps next month. There are bound to be differences in the nutrient profiles of these foods.

You will notice that several samples of each food were analyzed. There are variations in the content of individual samples and laboratory errors are possible. Using one or two samples would have involved less time and certainly less expense, but the findings would have been meaningless.

Chicken quarters, turkey wings and turkey thighs include the skin. Chicken carcasses are the body skeletons of chicken and do not include the skin.

To meet the needs of the laboratory, all samples were ground. By providing the samples in this condition, it was possible to receive quality analysis. The heaver/thicker part of bone was included with the thinner portion of bone to provide the average of six samples of every food.

Chicken Quarter (with skin) 100 gr. – as fed basis

TEST	MAX. VALUE	MIN. VALUE	MEAN	SAMPLE SIZE
Moisture %	63.33	57.65	60.51	6
Protein %	18.29	11.02	15.71	6
Calcium %	1.04	0.64	0.88	6
Phosphorus %	0.61	0.42	0.54	6
Sodium %	0.09	0.08	0.08	6
Potassium %	0.22	0.20	0.21	6
Magnesium %	0.04	0.03	0.03	6
Zinc (ppm)	23.97	12.77	17.85	6
Manganese (ppm)	‹1.0	‹1.0	‹1.0	6
Copper (ppm)	‹1.0	‹1.0	‹1.0	6
Iron (ppm)	28.37	15.88	20.62	6
Ash %	3.56	2.43	3.13	6
Fat %	24.17	18.65	21.19	6
Calories	289	212	254	6
Carbohydrates %	3.60	0	1.2	6

Chicken Carcass 100 gr. – as fed basis

TEST	MAX. VALUE	MIN. VALUE	MEAN	SAMPLE SIZE
Moisture %	63.43	60.62	62.34	6
Protein %	19.80	16.36	17.99	6
Calcium %	2.47	0.86	1.63	6
Phosphorus %	1.25	0.53	0.87	6
Sodium %	0.64	0.58	0.60	6
Potassium %	0.21	0.18	0.19	6
Magnesium %	0.06	0.03	0.04	6
Zinc (ppm)	29.06	18.87	22.85	6
Manganese (ppm)	<1.0	<1.0	<1.0	6
Copper (ppm)	<1.0	<1.0	<1.0	6
Iron (ppm)	22.40	18.52	19.89	6
Ash %	8.51	4.19	6.29	6
Fat %	17.74	9.81	14.45	6
Calories	231	167	202	6
Carbohydrates %	0.23	0	0.03	6

Lamb Shank 100 gr. – as fed basis

TEST	MAX. VALUE	MIN. VALUE	MEAN	SAMPLE SIZE
Moisture %	66.91	64.16	65.46	6
Protein %	28.80	20.23	23.23	6
Calcium %	1.54	1.01	1.24	6
Phosphorus %	0.83	0.61	0.70	6
Sodium %	0.12	0.09	0.10	6
Potassium %	0.32	0.29	0.30	6
Magnesium %	0.04	0.03	0.03	6
Zinc (ppm)	45.09	42.97	44.26	6
Manganese (ppm)	‹1.0	‹1.0	‹1.0	6
Copper (ppm)	‹1.0	‹1.0	‹1.0	6
Iron (ppm)	51.70	9.43	24.07	6
Ash %	5.08	3.73	4.29	6
Fat %	10.07	6.12	7.69	6
Calories	190	138	157	6
Carbohydrates %	0	0	0	6

Lamb Rib 100 gr. – as fed basis

TEST	MAX. VALUE	MIN. VALUE	MEAN	SAMPLE SIZE
Moisture %	54.00	49.21	51.51	6
Protein %	20.68	15.53	18.79	6
Calcium %	1.62	0.90	1.36	6
Phosphorus %	0.84	0.51	0.71	6
Sodium %	0.13	0.11	0.12	6
Potassium %	0.24	0.21	0.22	6
Magnesium %	0.04	0.03	0.03	6
Zinc (ppm)	42.66	31.31	35.25	6
Manganese (ppm)	‹1.0	‹1.0	‹1.0	6
Copper (ppm)	‹1.0	‹1.0	‹1.0	6
Iron (ppm)	12.87	11.89	12.43	6
Ash %	5.18	3.22	4.43	6
Fat %	28.67	24.24	26.27	6
Calories	340	280	311	6
Carbohydrates %	3.01	0	0.50	6

Pork Rib 100 gr. – as fed basis

TEST	MAX. VALUE	MIN. VALUE	MEAN	SAMPLE SIZE
Moisture %	58.91	53.83	56.64	6
Protein %	22.05	20.28	21.29	6
Calcium %	2.57	0.93	1.49	6
Phosphorus %	1.29	0.56	0.81	6
Sodium %	0.13	0.11	0.12	6
Potassium %	0.29	0.25	0.26	6
Magnesium %	0.06	0.03	0.04	6
Zinc (ppm)	27.30	25.12	26.44	6
Manganese (ppm)	<1.0	<1.0	<1.0	6
Copper (ppm)	<1.0	<1.0	<1.0	6
Iron (ppm)	20.86	14.55	17.60	6
Ash %	7.80	3.44	4.93	6
Fat %	24.11	19.18	21.51	6
Calories	298	259	279	6
Carbohydrates %	0	0	0	6

Turkey Wing 100 gr. – as fed basis

TEST	MAX. VALUE	MIN. VALUE	MEAN	SAMPLE SIZE
Moisture %	64.22	58.98	62.12	6
Protein %	27.31	19.17	22.58	6
Calcium %	3.31	1.48	2.09	6
Phosphorus %	1.62	0.80	1.07	6
Sodium %	0.14	0.11	0.12	6
Potassium %	0.24	0.21	0.22	6
Magnesium %	0.07	0.04	0.05	6
Zinc (ppm)	34.75	25.62	28.91	6
Manganese (ppm)	‹1.0	‹1.0	‹1.0	6
Copper (ppm)	‹1.0	‹1.0	‹1.0	6
Iron (ppm)	13.44	8.84	10.66	6
Ash %	9.80	4.70	6.44	6
Fat %	12.29	9.03	10.51	6
Calories	196	167	185	6
Carbohydrates %	1.57	0	0.26	6

Turkey Thigh 100 gr. – as fed basis

TEST	MAX. VALUE	MIN. VALUE	MEAN	SAMPLE SIZE
Moisture %	68.39	66.34	67.80	6
Protein %	20.71	20.14	20.35	6
Calcium %	1.27	0.03	0.74	6
Phosphorus %	0.76	0.21	0.53	6
Sodium %	0.11	0.09	0.10	6
Potassium %	0.33	0.30	0.31	6
Magnesium %	0.04	0.02	0.03	6
Zinc (ppm)	34.14	30.24	31.76	6
Manganese (ppm)	‹1.0	‹1.0	‹1.0	6
Copper (ppm)	‹1.0	‹1.0	‹1.0	6
Iron (ppm)	11.48	10.67	11.14	6
Ash %	4.41	1.16	3.02	6
Fat %	12.43	8.65	10.38	6
Calories	195	159	175	6
Carbohydrates %	0	0	0	6

Considerations

Minerals interact and we do not have life-long feeding trials of raw diets to review in a scientific fashion. This may or may not be a problem but it is something to consider. For example, in a previous chapter we discussed that excess calcium binds zinc, leaving some zinc unavailable to the body. Although raw meaty bones provide some zinc and, in fact, lamb seems to be an excellent source, calcium from the bones may leave at least some of the amount unavailable to the body. An excess or deficiency of one mineral can cause an avalanche of mineral interactions.

As we might expect from the raw meaty bone samples, calcium, phosphorus and magnesium are well balanced, so although these three minerals certainly interact, we can focus on what an excess of calcium may produce — interactions between zinc, copper and iron.

There have been claims that excess calcium fed in the form of raw meaty bones does not cause problems. Some people say that excess is excreted easily while calcium from other sources, such as bone meal, is not. This may be so but I have not found, nor has anyone come forward to show that this is anything but an hypothesis. In fact, my experience says that this is highly unlikely as evidenced by changing diets to include raw meaty bones in an amount to provide sufficient calcium without excess. When the diet was changed this way, problems presented to me as the reason for consultation resolved. These problems included poor skin and coat conditions, prolonged healing time after an injury or surgery, cracked foot pads and dry, cracked skin on the nose. All of these conditions may be attributed to a lack of zinc being absorbed and as suspected, reducing the amount of calcium in the diet increased zinc absorption and the problems resolved. For this reason, I would suggest that excess calcium from raw meaty bones is not excreted more easily than in any other form.

About the Supplements in These Diets

M OST OF THE FOLLOWING CHAPTERS address lifestyle and diseases and the dietary changes that may be helpful. Not all supplements are dietary per se. That is, they may not add to the vitamin or mineral profile of a diet. In these cases, a short discussion regarding these supplements is included but they are not included in the actual diet. Nevertheless, adding them could be helpful. For instance, taurine is mentioned in the chapter about heart disease but is not included in diet plans.

Where supplements are included in diet plans, it is recognized that some people may not have access to certain brands. For this reason, you should know what supplements contain so that you can find a comparable brand. Understand that using supplements with different nutrient profiles from those below will change the nutrient profile of the entire diet.

· One teaspoon bone meal: 660 mg calcium, 280 mg phosphorus (or may be replaced by ¾ teaspoon of another bone meal that provides 900 mg calcium and 450 mg phosphorus)

· One teaspoon di-calcium phosphate: 1,025 mg calcium, 900 mg phosphorus

· One teaspoon NOW® Calcium Carbonate Powder: 1,200 mg calcium

· Vitamin A (depends on source): 1 retinol equivalent in micrograms (1 mcg RE) is equal to 6 IU from beta-carotense *or* 4.1 IU from milk or yogurt *or* 3.33 IU from animal sources and fortified foods

· One tablet vitamin B compound: 50 mcg B-12, 50 mg of all other B vitamins

· Vitamin D: 200 IU = 5 mcg

- Vitamin E: 1 IU = 0.67 mg d-alpha tocopherol
- One teaspoon kelp: 3,000 mg iodine
- One capsule cod liver oil: 1,250 IU vitamin A and 100 IU vitamin D
- One capsule Allergy Research MultiMin™: 83 mg calcium, 6 mg iron, 83 mg magnesium, 10 mg zinc, 33 mcg selenium, 0.5 mg copper, 5 mg manganese, 133 mcg chromium, 83 mcg molybdenum, 33 mg potassium, 333 mcg boron, 67 mcg vanadium, 67 mg glutamic acid
- One capsule Allergy Research Multi-Vi-Min®: 4,000 IU vitamin A, 20 mg vitamin B1, 10 mg vitamin B2, 30 mg vitamin B3, 100 mg vitamin B5, 31 mg vitamin B6, 60 mcg folic acid, 80 mcg vitamin B-12, 80 mcg biotin, 100 IU vitamin D, 80 IU vitamin E, 50 mg calcium, 50 mg magnesium, 0.20 mg potassium, 0.30 mg copper, 4 mg iron, 3 mg manganese, 40 mcg selenium

About Feeding Supplements

Bone meal, di-calcium phosphate, kelp and generic calcium can be added to food before the meals are frozen for future use. They are quite stable and will not be affected by temperature changes.

Oils and vitamin E are light and heat sensitive and are best added to meals before feeding.

B vitamins and multivitamins and multi-minerals can upset empty stomachs. Always give them with food. The best way to do this is to tuck them in a hand-held piece of food and feed as a treat. Do not add them to food before freezing.

Where B vitamins are noted as feeding one tablet per week, cut a tablet and give one quarter as required to arrive at a full tablet over a seven day period. B vitamins are water-soluble and, other than B-12, which circulates in the body for one month, should be supplied often.

CHAPTER 9
Lifestyle

O UR PUPPIES HAVE GROWN into healthy, happy adult dogs. They have now celebrated their third birthdays. They live very different lifestyles and bring unique challenges to their owners.

The Couch Potato
Jackson turned out to be the couch potato his breeder had anticipated. His activities include one daily walk outdoors and following his owner around the house in hope of receiving a treat. His owner spoils him, and as a result, Jackson has gained more weight than what the veterinarian deems healthy. He weighs forty-two pounds and should weigh forty. There are three ways of accomplishing this two-pound weight loss.

1. More exercise
2. Less food
3. A combination of both of the above

The third method is the best because exercise is important for general health, but eating less food will help to speed up weight loss. Muscles burn more calories than body fat does. By providing more exercise, muscle mass can increase and Jackson should be able to consume more food than if he were on a weight loss diet. An added bonus is that exercise benefits the heart, lungs and lean muscle mass. Jackson's owner is recovering from a health problem that does not allow her to walk him quickly or more than once a day. She will increase his activity by playing fetch with him in the backyard or indoors. He will have to work for a treat rather than being fed one simply because he wants it. Asking Jackson to sit, lie down and sit again is like a "doggie sit-up." After a few repetitions he will be rewarded, sometimes with a food treat but more often with praise and belly rubs. Food treats will be reduced in size by half and fed less often. At least 25% of these treats will be baby carrots and green beans rather than calorie-laden baked goodies. Reducing the amount of food in Jackson's bowl also reduces the amounts of protein, fat, carbohydrates, vitamins and minerals he receives. Although he needs fewer calories, his body requires nutrients based on his ideal weight. To calculate this, his owner uses the following guide written by Christine Zink, DVM, PhD.

Caloric Recommendations by Weight and Activity Level

DOG'S WEIGHT (in pounds)	INACTIVE	MODERATELY ACTIVE	HIGHLY ACTIVE
10	234	303	441
20	373	483	702
30	489	633	921
40	593	768	1,117
50	689	892	1,297
60	779	1,008	1,466
70	863	1,222	1,777
90	1,022	1,322	1,923
100	1,097	1,419	2,064

Figures represent the average number of calories required daily to maintain the dog's weight. The figures include daily calories from all sources, including treats and snacks. Metabolism can vary greatly. It is not unusual for the caloric needs of dogs with the same weight and lifestyle to vary by up to 20%. The chart above is merely a starting point. After looking at this guideline, Jackson's owner recognizes that the diet should provide about 768 kilocalories. His current diet provides 850 kilocalories daily — an excess of 82 kilocalories per day. There are 3,500 kilocalories in one pound. Jackson needs to lose two pounds, equivalent to 7,000 kilocalories. By reducing his caloric intake by 82 kilocalories per day, we can expect him to shed the unwanted pounds in 85 days if his activity level remains the same. However, since Jackson will be getting more exercise, he is likely to lose weight faster. If his new exercise regime continues after he reaches his ideal weight, he will probably require a few more kilocalories per day to maintain a healthy weight from that point on.

The Show Dog

Travis has been working the show ring with enthusiasm. His good health, wonderful temperament and multiple championships have prompted other breeders to want to use him often. Travis has been busy!

This busy lifestyle includes the stress of travel, being handled by different people in the ring, meeting many other dogs and of course, being used at stud on a fairly constant basis. While this 42-pound dog may be having fun, he is also under stress, and stress can bring on oxidative damage.

His owner/breeder is also feeling stressed because Travis needs to be in top-notch condition at all times to meet everyone's expectations.

Diet can play an important role in helping the show dog.

Travis' Weekly Cooked Diet

14 ounces ground beef, lean, 15% fat

1 ¾ ounces beef liver

36 ounces potatoes, with skin, boiled

7 eggs, large, hard boiled

4 ounces sockeye salmon with bones, canned, drained

11 ounces ground pork

20 ounces turkey breast with skin

1 apple, raw

1 banana, raw

14 baby carrots, raw (used as treats)

3 ounces zucchini

2 ounces rice, brown, raw

7 capsules, vitamin E 200 IU

12 teaspoons bone meal

½ teaspoon kelp

5 capsules, Allergy Research MultiMin™

7,000 milligrams wild salmon oil

30 milligrams zinc

100 milligrams magnesium

This cooked diet provides 726 kilocalories per day that break down as 36% from protein, 25% from carbohydrates and 39% from fat.

Unless otherwise noted, all weights, other than the raw rice and baby carrots, are the yield after foods have been cooked. In addition to the items listed, 250 milligrams of taurine daily would ensure that Travis is receiving an ample amount of this amino acid to help heart function. While Travis enjoys the variety in his diet when he is at home, this very popular show dog spends quite a bit of time on the road. His professional handlers are not expected to cook for him, so Travis eats a high quality kibble when he travels. His owner weans him off the home-cooked food and onto kibble at least one week before any travel time. This allows the digestive system to adjust to dietary changes and prevents dramatic gut reactions while on the road. Travis continues to receive raw fruits, baby carrots, wild salmon oil, vitamin E and taurine while away from home. His owner weans him back onto a home-prepared diet once he returns.

The Canine Athlete

Beamer loves agility trials and does very well. His body is a lean machine that requires the same healthy nutrition as other dogs. However, because he is well-muscled and uses a lot of energy, his caloric requirements are greater than those of the average 40-pound dog. Oxidative damage can occur more often in hard-working dogs, so his diet should be fortified with antioxidants. Athletes are also more likely to experience muscle strains and damage.

A decline in plasma ascorbate in sled dogs during the racing season was largely prevented by ascorbic acid dietary supplements. Supplementing with vitamin C also may help racing dogs by facilitating oxidation of fatty acids by mitochondria in working muscles.[18]

Another study of sled dogs found that dogs with higher plasma concentrations of vitamin E had greater endurance than dogs with lower concentrations.[19] This does not to translate to a dog running faster, but endurance is an important consideration for agility.

Beamer is certainly not working as hard as a sled dog, and supplementing his diet with vitamin C should be done with caution since it can put him at risk for calcium oxalate problems. His owner is willing to

18 *The Waltham Book of Clinical Nutrition of the Dog and Cat* (1994).
19 Piercy, R. J., Hinchcliff, K. W., Morley, P. S., Disilvstro, R. A., Reinhart, G. A., Nelson, S. L. Jr., Schmidt, K. E., Morrie, C. A. (May 2001) Association between vitamin E and enhanced athletic performance in sled dogs. *Medicine & Science in Sports & Exercise;* 33 (5): 826-833.

take the risk and supplementing with 250 milligrams of Ester-C® daily. In addition, Beamer consumes fruits and vegetables that provide vitamin C and the added benefits of phytonutrients.

About Phytonutrients

Phytonutrients, sometimes referred to as phytochemicals, are naturally-occurring compounds in vegetables, fruits, legumes and whole grains. They contribute to the color, flavor and disease resistance of plants. Science has focused on phytonutrients and found that most act as antioxidants that are helpful to humans by preventing tumors, enhancing immunity and strengthening heart and blood vessels. The role of phytonutrients is increasing as science tries to catch up to Mother Nature.

For instance, lycopene is a red pigment found in high amounts in tomatoes. Lycopene is recognized as being important for eye health and also acts as an antioxidant that may prevent certain forms of cancer. Anthocyanins are phytonutrients that give fruits and vegetables their red, blue or purple color. There is some evidence that anthocyanins have anti-inflammatory properties as well as acting as antioxidants.

Beta-carotene is a phytonutrient carotenoid with antioxidant and provitamin A activity. In addition to its other roles, it works with other natural protectors to defend cells from harmful free radical damage. This is important because beta-carotene plays a role in recovery from exercise and other stresses.

The study of phytochemicals is incomplete and will probably take many more years before recommended allowances or doses can be provided. Knowledge of their composition, the effect of heating these compounds, whether or not particular ones are absorbed, how much is absorbed, and correlation to disease and disease prevention is in its infancy.[20]

We are using current knowledge to hedge our bets in the case of Beamer's diet. We know that as a working dog, he can probably make good use of antioxidants and phytonutrients so his diet provides both.

---

20 Wrolstad, R. E., Distinguished Professor Emeritus of Food Science and Technology, Oregon State University, Corvallis, OR. Private conversation.

Beamer's Weekly Raw Diet

7 ounces lamb rib, ground

6 ounces turkey wing

4 ounces turkey neck

1 ¼ ounces beef liver

46 ounces ground turkey

4 eggs, large, without shells

16 ounces beef heart

10 ounces chicken giblets

5 oysters, canned

3 ounces zucchini

24 ounces sweet potato

3 ounces broccoli

3 ounces carrot

2 bananas

3 ounces cantaloupe

2 ounces blueberries

½ teaspoon kelp

450 milligrams magnesium citrate

10 milligrams manganese

7 capsules, vitamin E 200 IU

7,000 milligrams wild salmon oil

7 capsules, cod liver oil

This raw diet provides 762 kilocalories per day that break down as 38% from protein, 20% from carbohydrates and 42% from fat.

Beamer will not be fed a very heavy meal before he performs. Instead, his owner will give him a small amount of raw meaty bones, eggs or meat combined with sweet potatoes.

Beamer will need small amounts of food to support his need for quick energy and hydration throughout the day. Fruits, dehydrated sweet potato slices and small amounts of meat will be used as treats. His owner makes dehydrated treats at home to take on the road. She sets the oven to 275 degrees and thinly slices bananas, sweet potatoes and pork heart into strips and places them in a single layer on a cookie sheet lined with parchment paper. In about one hour, she has convenient and mess-free treats for Beamer. Extras can be kept in the refrigerator for up to five days.

Hydrating the Working Dog

Many of my clients have performance and working dogs. Although they are very concerned about providing proper nutrition, their number one question seems to be how to ensure their dogs drink enough.

Most dogs that eat a home-prepared diet do not drink nearly as much as those that eat bagged foods, because fresh food contains at least 70% moisture. Still, hard-working animals need to be well hydrated to perform well. Dehydration can cause fatigue, poor performance, weakness, muscle cramping, decreased coordination and therefore injury. In addition, dehydration can cause the heart to work harder in an effort to move blood through the bloodstream and risks overheating. So how much is enough and when should you start to worry?

The amount of fluid required to rehydrate depends quite a bit on how much fluid the dog has lost. To get a better idea of what might work for your dog, weigh him/her before and after workouts. The difference is mostly water so that is about how much liquid your dog should be putting back in the body during the course of the exercise.

Now that you have a goal, you may also have a challenge in getting your dog to drink this amount. Sports drinks for dogs seem to be the latest craze. Most contain added color and/or preservatives. Dogs do not need these expensive designer waters, but they do like water with some flavor. The most successful way to do this is by offering meat-based broths with a pinch of salt. Make a lean broth by boiling meat and/or bones in a pot of water. Once cooked, strain the broth and place it in the refrigerator overnight. Remove any fat that has risen and congealed on top. Pour the broth into ice cube trays. Place frozen cubes in a travel bag and place the bag in a cooler packed with ice. Offer your dog the frozen cubes or allow the cubes to melt and offer the broth between exercise sessions.

Grains for the Working Dog

Feeding grains to dogs has fallen out of favor over the last few years. One of the many arguments against it is that grains are not a natural food for dogs. Indeed, they are not. Then again, neither are the joint supplements being fed to canine athletes or the kelp being fed to most dogs on home-prepared diets. Certainly, expecting a dog to literally jump through hoops or walk down a teeter-totter or weave through poles could be considered unnatural as well.

I like feeding some grains to working dogs and make no apology for it. Grains provide carbohydrates that work as quick fuel for the bursts of energy required. Unlike protein and fat, which take longer to be converted into energy, carbohydrates feed the muscles and brain for a quicker reaction when needed. Working dogs that eat carbohydrates can more easily perform and sustain their energy levels better. As a bonus, grains tend to be a fairly good source of selenium and manganese. Selenium works with iodine for thyroid health and manganese works together with other minerals to promote joint health.

Am I promoting grain-based diets? Not at all. Dogs are certainly capable of utilizing the nutrients in grains, but we are feeding canines, not herbivores. That said, a few baked treats that include oats or flours can be helpful when a dog needs a quick energy boost. Including a little grain in the morning meal before the sports event can make a positive difference to your dog's performance.

Beamer eats a few of the following treats at every sporting event. They provide quick energy without adding grains to his weekly diet.

Beamer's Favorite Cookies

1 cup whole wheat flour

1 cup rye flour

1 teaspoon NOW® Calcium Carbonate Powder (1,200 milligrams calcium)

2 teaspoons fennel greens, finely chopped or 1 teaspoon fennel seeds

1 small clove garlic, minced

¼ cup chicken broth

Preparation: Combine all dry ingredients in a bowl. Add chicken broth. Mix well. Dough will be very stiff. If necessary, add a little more chicken broth. Place dough on a floured board. Cut in eight pieces. Roll each piece into a log, about 1" in diameter. Slice into cookies, ⅛" thick each. Place cookies on a non-stick cookie sheet and bake in preheated 300 degree oven for 1 hour or until golden. Turn oven off and allow cookies to cool down in the oven so they dry to a very hard biscuit.

Supplements for the Working Dog

If my experience is any indication, there are probably more supplements being fed to working dogs than to any other healthy pets. When working with clients who own these animals, I usually see a long list of supplements being fed on a regular basis. Owners feel they help to prevent injuries in working dogs. When a dog has been injured, even more supplements are added. How necessary is this, and more to the point, how effective are supplements for prevention and cure? Are supplements being fed as a substitute for a truly balanced diet?

The fact is, when a diet meets the dog's nutrient requirements, few supplements are needed. In almost all cases, when a diet falls short, a multivitamin and mineral or a multi-mineral complex will be all that is required. The only exception is in the case of very sensitive animals that do not tolerate certain forms form or formulations of vitamins and/or minerals. In that case, we can supplement in different ways.

The working dog has four main challenges: maintaining skeletal health, sustained energy expenditure, maintaining hydration and reducing inflammation. Joint supportive supplements can be helpful if a dog sustains certain injuries.

Maintaining skeletal health should not be the ordeal it is sometimes made out to be. In fact, left to their own devices, most canines are athletic by nature. In my opinion, the problem is not so much what the dog can do, but rather, that we sometimes expect more of them than their individual structure will allow. Ensuring your dog has a sound skeletal system is essential to preventing injury. Expecting supplements to compensate for poor structure is simply unrealistic.

Glucosamine is an organic compound found in cartilage and joint fluid. Glucosamine supplements can help support joints but has not been proven to prevent joints from wearing down. As an example, while it can reduce arthritis pain, it will not prevent arthritis.

The efficacy of chondroiten is debatable. Some people say it cannot possibly do any good because its molecules are too large to be absorbed. Others say that chondroiten helps. My experience is that chondroiten alone is not helpful, but supplements that combine it with glucosamine work better than glucosamine alone. Chondroiten sulfate is recommended over other forms.

MSM (methylsulfonylmethane) is a sulfur compound found in fresh fruits and vegetables, milk, fish and grains, but it is quickly destroyed when foods are processed. Its efficacy is controversial. Studies have found that MSM eased rheumatoid arthritis-like symptoms in mice and prolonged life for mice with a condition similar to lupus nephritis. Nothing has been proven in regard to people or dogs, but people report pain relief when using products containing MSM. The best results I see in dogs come from products that contain glucosamine, chondroiten and MSM in one formulation.

Fish oils have antinflammatory properties. This is one supplement that I believe in giving dogs daily (unless the diet is already based on fatty fish). The added bonus is that fish oil provides omega-3 fatty acids, which promote heart health as well. My oil of choice is wild salmon oil.

CoQ10, also known as ubiquinone, is a powerful antioxidant. According to some studies, it protects tissues in the heart and other vital organs from free radical damage, produces energy in cells and strengthens the immune system. High quality CoQ10 is relatively expensive and should not be considered vital as a supplement for any dog. The few studies conducted on dogs have focused on heart health alone, and CoQ10 proved to be a disappointment in this regard. Still, it may have its place as an important antioxidant. I do not consider a CoQ10 supplement to be essential by any means, but I have used it to help some canine athletes and have witnessed anecdotal evidence that it is helpful for promoting energy.

In a nutshell, a canine athlete needs a healthy diet including antioxidants, and (unless the diet provides plenty of fatty fish) the addition of omega-3 fatty acids. It is a simple, inexpensive plan that does not clutter your shelves with bottles of supplements.

Chapter Summary

· Weight loss is best achieved by increasing activity and decreasing caloric intake.

· Feed enough calories to support the dog's ideal weight rather than drastically reducing calories for very quick weight loss.

· Change a feeding method over 5–7 days to reduce the risk of digestive upset.

· Phytonutrients play important roles.

· Grains are a good source of carbohydrates. They provide a quick energy boost and some selenium and manganese.

· Hydration is key to performance.

· Supplements are not a substitute for a good diet.

CHAPTER 10
Heart Disease

J ACKSON GAINED BACK THE TWO POUNDS that he lost a short while ago. He is more active than in the past so, the weight gain is mostly muscle mass. The veterinarian has diagnosed Jackson with a heart murmur and dilated cardiomyopathy, a condition in which the heart is weakened, becomes enlarged, and cannot pump blood efficiently. This decreased heart function can affect the lungs, liver and other body systems.

Some heart problems are genetic. Although valvular problems can be found in many breeds, the Cavalier King Charles Spaniel is the poster dog for mitral valve disease. Dilated cardiomyopathy is found in many breeds including Boxers, Doberman Pinchers, Great Danes, Irish Wolfhounds, American Cocker Spaniels, Saint Bernards and German Shepherd Dogs.

Some valvular problems may be related to a lack of collagen and elastin. No dietary measures seem to help these cases, but the heart, forced to try and compensate for the valve problem, may benefit from certain supplements.

To begin, we will review amino acids. Proteins are chains of amino acids. The body can manufacture some amino acids and also combine them to create others. Of the list of amino acids, those that the body can make for itself are called non-essential and those that must come from food, are called essential.Among other roles, taurine and carnitine are important to heart health. The body produces taurine by combining cysteine and methionine. Carnitine, although described as an amino acid, is in fact a substance related to the B vitamin group. Its main function is fatty acid transport rather than protein synthesis. The body manufactures carnitine by combining methionine and lysine. Meats, especially heart, and other foods of animal origin are also good sources of carnitine.

Classification of Amino Acids for Dogs

ESSENTIAL	NON-ESSENTIAL
Arginine	Alanine
Histidine	Asparagine
Isoleucine	Aspartic Acid
Leucine	Cysteine
Lysine	Glutamic Acid
Methionine	Glutamine
Phenylalanine	Glycine
Threonine	Proline
Tryptophan	Serine
Valine	Tyrosine

Since the body requires methionine and lysine, both essential amino acids, to produce taurine and carnitine, you might wonder if Jackson's diet lacked them. It did not; in fact, it would be very difficult to produce a meat-based diet that did.

Would adding taurine and carnitine supplements to Jackson's diet be beneficial? A taurine supplement could help and certainly would not hurt. Since the discovery that certain breeds have a taurine deficiency, many dog food manufacturers having been adding this amino acid to their formulations. While this may or may not apply to home-prepared diets, it is reasonable to ensure that dogs are not missing out on something so important. Current thinking suggests the following addition:

· *Small Dogs:* 125 milligrams taurine per day

· *Medium Dogs:* 250 milligrams taurine per day

· *Large Dogs:* 500 milligrams taurine per day

· *Giant Breeds:* 1 gram taurine per day

Adding supplemental carnitine to the diet is a debatable approach. Most veterinarians agree it is probably not beneficial. There is no correlation between the amount of carnitine circulating in the blood and the amount in the heart muscle. A heart biopsy would reveal deficiency, but obviously, this is not an approach that the dog or pet owner would welcome.

Supplemental carnitine is expensive to use in the amounts needed to show any effect, if indeed it has any. In the case of dilated cardiomyopathy, if carnitine is helping, improvement may be seen on an echocardiogram in 8 – 12 weeks. Echocardiography also shows that a plateau may be reached after 6 – 8 months of supplementation.

The recommended oral dose for L-carnitine is 50 – 100 mg/kg body weight three times daily.[21]

Sodium and Potassium
Kidney function includes the ability to excrete water and sodium. This excretion provides control of blood pressure. In the case of some heart diseases, and certainly in congestive heart failure, the kidneys lose some of their ability to excrete sodium well. This results in sodium retention that, in turn, results in water retention. One noticeable symptom of this in dogs is coughing. A radiograph would probably show fluid retention in the lungs.

Typically, one of the first reactions of pet owners who learn their dog has any form of heart disease is to want to decrease the sodium content of the diet. Although this may apply to dry and canned foods because they tend to provide a lot of sodium, in the case of home-prepared diets, there is less cause for concern because fresh foods without added salt provide the least amount of sodium possible. That said, some foods contain less sodium than others. For example, canned fish could be eliminated altogether, ricotta cheese could replace cottage cheese and some RMBs provide more sodium than others.

Is the focus on sodium as important as we think? It is not critical in the early stages of heart disease and, in fact, restricting it too much can cause problems. Sodium is an important mineral, and a very low-sodium diet triggers the body to try and conserve it using a hormonal gatekeeper called aldosterone. The possible problem lies in the fact that aldosterone is also responsible for triggering the kidneys to excrete potassium. If a dog loses too much potassium, it will feel ill and weak and may lose balance.

With heart failure comes the risk of fat and skeletal muscle loss. This condition is known as cardiac cachexia and is due to lessened appetite, increased energy need, medications used for heart disease and poor

21 Hand, M. S., Thatcher, C. D., Remillard, R. L., Roudebush, P. (2000) *Small Animal Clinical Nutrition*, 4th Edition.

assimilation of food. Drastic reduction in sodium can make food taste less appealing and as the dog eats less, muscle wasting develops while the amount of potassium ingested also drops.

Treatment for heart disease usually involves medications that can take their toll on the kidneys. For this reason and because compromised heart function can affect kidney function, it makes sense to feed a diet that is friendly to both.

If Jackson had kidney disease, we would lower phosphorus. Since he does not, we should not lower phosphorus dramatically as this could cause more harm. We will continue to feed him foods with high-quality protein and use wild salmon oil as an important supplement, as it is both kidney and heart friendly (note that plant based oils do not help compromised kidneys).

Jackson's Weekly, Heart Friendly Combination Diet

24 ½ ounces ground beef, 20% fat

2 ½ ounces beef liver

49 ¼ ounces rabbit, with organs, headless

2 ounces zucchini

56 ounces potato, without skin, boiled

7 capsules, vitamin E 200 IU

½ teaspoon kelp

10,500 milligrams wild salmon oil

7 capsules, cod liver oil

5 capsules, Allergy Research MultiMin™

20 milligrams zinc

12 ½ milligrams B complex (¼ of a 50 milligram tablet)

This combination diet provides 733 kilocalories per day that break down as 32% from protein, 26% from carbohydrates and 42% from fat. It provides sodium at 88% of the recommended allowance.

Remember that Jackson weighs 42 pounds and he is no longer a couch potato. If he needed to consume more or less of this diet, nutrient values would increase or decrease accordingly. Potatoes contain little sodium, are a good source of potassium, and like other carbohydrates, have a protein sparing effect on the body. In the case of heart disease, where muscle wastage can become a problem and excessive potassium excretion may also occur, potatoes can make a positive impact.

Weekly, Heart Friendly Cooked Diet

25 ounces ground beef, 25% fat, baked

16 ounces chicken breast with skin, stewed

1 ½ ounces beef liver, fried

44 ounces white rice, long grain

¾ cup zucchini, boiled, no salt

6,000 milligrams wild salmon oil

7 capsules, vitamin E 100 IU

4 capsules, cod liver oil

¼ teaspoon kelp

8 teaspoons bone meal

2 capsules, Allergy Research MultiMin™

1 ½ teaspoons No-Salt®

300 milligrams magnesium citrate

15 milligrams zinc

12 ¼ milligrams vitamin B compound (¼ of a 50 milligram tablet)

This cooked diet should support the weight of a moderately active 25-pound dog. It provides 632 kilocalories per day that break down as 32% from protein, 33% from carbohydrates and 35% from fat. Provides sodium at 73% of the recommended allowance and so, is more suitable for later stages of heart failure.

Note to the reader: All weights and measures are the yield; the amount a food weighs or measures after cooking.

Chapter Summary

· Supplemental taurine may be helpful.

· Supplemental carnitine is controversial.

· Restriction of dietary sodium is not necessary in early stages of heart disease and, in fact, may negatively impact the status of potassium.

· Restrict sodium in later stages of heart disease by choosing lower-sodium foods (USDA provides mineral values of commonly fed foods).

· Include wild salmon oil in the diet for its heart and kidney friendly benefits.

· Ensure the diet provides enough potassium.

CHAPTER 11
Liver Disease

Z ACH'S OWNER ENJOYS HUNTING and often takes the dog with him on these outdoor excursions. Zach has made a few canine friends during his time in the field, including Logan, his favorite buddy. Unfortunately, Logan's blood test results have shown a steady rise in liver enzymes. He has undergone a liver biopsy and is recuperating at home. The good news is that Logan does not have a copper retention disorder. His diet will be able to include a normal amount of copper.

Infection or a toxic load being dealt with by the liver can cause elevations in liver enzymes. Liver shunts, copper storage disease, chronic hepatitis and a host of other problems can also affect liver function. Sometimes the problem is genetic.

Supporting liver function through dietary changes can show positive results, but a definitive diagnosis is first required. This sometimes entails a biopsy. Without a diagnosis, nutritional management may be unreliable.

Like their owners, dogs are unique. Not all dogs will have the same manifestation of the same disease. Not all dogs will respond equally to the same diet.

Most of the studies that focus on naturally-occurring liver disease are based on experiments that induced the disease in animals or gathered from literature that focuses on people. This is one of many reasons for appreciating that naturally occurring liver disease may be looked at differently than other causes of compromised liver function.

What's Really Happening?

Although the liver has many important functions, one of the most stressful is the elimination of protein byproducts. This might lead us to believe that feeding less protein would be helpful but, in fact, the liver requires protein for regeneration. The key is to offer proteins of high biological value that leave less "waste" for the liver to dispose of.

The tissue break down (catabolism) that liver patients experience tends to increase caloric requirements. The body uses protein and fat for energy production. Proteins are broken down at an increased rate while absorption is decreased. This is what lies behind a need to ensure that adequate amounts of protein are being fed and that the biological value of the foods is high.

One of the many roles of the liver is to produce cholesterol and other fats called phospholipids. However, compromised liver function does not necessitate a low-fat diet. Dogs with experimentally induced portosystemic shunt (which results in abnormal blood flow in the liver) have almost normal fat utilization, so it is not considered necessary to restrict fats in the diet of most patients. That said, we do not want to feed too much fat. High-fat diets are not tolerated well by some dogs and will not help the ones with liver disease. Fat plays key roles (increases a dog's likelihood to consume more food, provides essential fatty acids, has protein sparing effects and offers added calories), but should not be fed to an extreme.

Dietary Guidelines

Urea is the chief end product of protein metabolism. The liver plays a key role in the detoxification of ammonia to urea. Red meats are highly ammongenic and should be eliminated or greatly reduced when liver function is compromised. However, restriction of protein in general can cause the body to try and use its own muscle protein. This not only weakens the body but also has an effect similar to feeding red meat.[22]

The breakdown of amino acids for energy is minimized by the consumption of carbohydrates. Fiber helps to slow down the absorption of carbohydrates and reduces the absorption and even the availability of some bacterial toxins and bile acids. Carbohydrates also have a protein-sparing effect: they reduce glucagon release, so that amino acids absorbed

---

22 Leveille-Webster, C. R., Tufts University School of Veterinary Medicine (Sep 2002) *Tufts Animal Expo Conference Proceedings*, Boston, MA.

from the intestine are converted to protein instead of to glucose. A combination of simple and complex carbohydrates seems to work best. Highly digestible options are white rice, potatoes and vegetables.

Isoleucine, leucine and valine are called branch chain amino acids. The ratio between these and other amino acids, and the fact that branch chain amino acids are, theoretically, very friendly to the liver, makes them worth noting. However, clinical trials have not been able to show consistent results. Providing sufficient protein seems to be more significant than focusing on branch chain amino acids.

My personal experience differs from controlled trials. My clients have seen positive results when fish, cheese or yogurt is the main protein source in a diet, as these foods are great sources of branch chain amino acids. W. Jean Dodds, DVM, has seen the same results when her clients feed a home-prepared fish based diet. However, the explanation may not be this simplistic. The diets also include a relatively large amount of potato and some have included white rice. The combination seems to work extremely well.

Some dogs with liver disease experience nausea and eat less as a result. By consuming less food, they are also ingesting fewer nutrients. B vitamins are water-soluble. The body excretes them through urine. Red meats are a good source of B vitamins, but they are often eliminated or reduced in a diet for liver disease. This may cause a deficiency. For these reasons, supplementing the diet with a B vitamin complex makes sense.

Vitamin E is a fat-soluble vitamin and powerful antioxidant. Fat-soluble vitamins may be deficient in cases of bile acid deficiency. A vitamin E supplement should be added to all diets but becomes even more important in these cases.

Feeding a few meals per day, rather than just one or two, can be very helpful. Smaller amounts of food results in less bacterial fermentation at any one time, and therefore less for the liver to deal with. Feeding several small meals per day can also be more comfortable for the dog since the stomach is not so full at meal time and the animal feels less nauseous. Slightly nauseated animals may not want to eat as much at each meal, but may still end up eating a full ration by the end of the day if several small meals are fed.

Zinc and Copper

Unfortunately, most of the home-prepared diets that I have analyzed are deficient in zinc, but, just as unfortunately, many people decide to supplement this mineral as soon as a dog is diagnosed with liver disease. This is unacceptable without the guidance of a veterinarian to monitor the dog. While zinc deficiency impairs many functions including those involved with detoxification, zinc interferes with iron absorption.

Supplementation with copper alone should be avoided, because some cases of liver disease may affect proper copper excretion. The liver stores copper and can be adversely affected by adding a copper supplement. Further, copper interacts with zinc and iron.

A balanced diet that includes all minerals is important, and a multimineral that includes copper and zinc may be added to the diet unless a dog has been diagnosed with copper retention. The key is in knowing how much of any given mineral food sources provide, and then supplementing only as needed to meet a dog's requirements while understanding that requirements change as health conditions change.

Sample Diets

I prefer to feed liver-compromised dogs a cooked diet for the following reason: in most cases, a liver biopsy is not performed unless the situation is critical or mystifying enough to warrant further investigation. Also, the more commonly performed punch biopsy is not as diagnostic as a full biopsy. This means an owner may have to feed a dog that has been diagnosed with nothing more specific than elevated liver enzymes for some time. Nevertheless, the owner needs to make feeding decisions right away. Given the possibility of infection, it is prudent to feed cooked foods to a compromised animal.

With that said, I am a realist. Your dog is your responsibility, and you may still feel that a raw diet is best. For those who prefer to feed a raw diet, a modified diet plan is included below.

Weekly, Liver Friendly Cooked Diet

28 ounces cod, baked

21 ounces ricotta cheese

10 large eggs, hardboiled

42 ounces potato, peeled, boiled

1 ounce carrot, cooked

50 milligrams B vitamin compound
7 capsules, vitamin E 100 IU
3 ½ teaspoons bone meal
1 ½ teaspoons NOW® Calcium Carbonate Powder
4 capsules, Allergy Research MultiMin™
20 milligrams zinc citrate or gluconate
3 milligrams copper, chelated
¼ teaspoon kelp

This cooked diet provides 527 kilocalories per day and breaks down as 36% from protein, 29% from carbohydrates and 35% from fat. It should support the weight of a 19-pound dog.

Weekly, Liver Friendly Combination Diet

22 ounces turkey thigh
12 large eggs without shells
20 ounces whole milk yogurt
36 ounces sweet potato, raw
16 ounces zucchini, raw
3 ½ canned oysters
12 ounces cod, baked
36 ounces ground turkey
½ teaspoon kelp
1 large eggshell, ground
5 capsules, Allergy Research MultiMin™
50 milligrams B compound
7 capsules, vitamin E 200 IU
6 milligrams copper, chelated

This combination diet provides 698 kilocalories per day that break down as 40% from protein, 21% from carbohydrates and 39% from fat. It should support the weight of a relatively inactive 40-pound dog.

The cooked fish and canned oysters are what make this a combination diet rather than a fully raw one. While healthy dogs may be able to combat the parasites that raw fish can contain, a compromised animal is at greater risk. Raw oysters can carry an organism like one found in raw pacific-northwest salmon. It can kill a dog.

Supplements for Liver Support

Supporting the natural antioxidant systems of the body makes even more sense when we consider that the liver is a main site of this process. Oral supplementation with taurine and vitamin E has proven to be beneficial for maintaining natural antioxidant systems.[23]

There are also many scientific studies indicating that the herb milk thistle is beneficial for the liver. Its effects include decreasing liver and bile cholesterol, reducing inflammation, protecting liver tissue, limiting damage from disrupted oxygen supply and helping to regenerate damaged liver tissue.

Milk thistle contains silymarin, a compound that scavenges free radicals and silybin, which counteract or prevent liver damage from many toxins. This herb has been proven to be very safe and most dogs tolerate it quite well.

The downside to most milk thistle is that it can taste very bitter, so adding it to a meal is very likely to make the dog walk away from the food dish. Give it in capsule form or in a loose powder that has been tested and proven not to be bitter. Liquid forms do not seem to be more acceptable to dogs than the powdered versions. Feeding too much milk thistle can cause nausea and/or loosen stool. Most reactions are temporary. Let your dog adjust slowly and increase the amount as needed over a period of several days while observing the dog's reaction.

SAMe is another supplement that may be helpful. The body is nothing short of a miracle network. Everything in it is connected. Things become more fascinating and intricate at the cellular level. A compromised liver is no exception, and, while it would be easier to direct you to use SAMe in these cases, it is important that you understand why.

SAMe (S-adenosyl L-methionine) is a naturally-occuring substance. It plays many key roles, including serving as a precursor for cysteine, one of the three amino acids of glutathione. The precursor of SAMe is methio-

---

23 Scanlan, N., American Holistic Veterinary Medical Association (Sept 2001) Compromised hepatic detoxification in companion animals and its correction via nutritional supplementation and modified fasting; *Alternative Medicine Review*; 6 Suppl: S24-37.

nine, an essential amino acid. One of the consequences of liver disease is that the activity of this amino acid is greatly decreased. Administration of this innocuous supernutrient results in many beneficial effects in various tissues, mainly in the liver, and especially in the mitochondria. This was shown in alcohol-fed baboons and in other experimental models of liver injury and in clinical trials.[24]

Chapter Summary

· Liver disease can be caused by many different factors.

· Dietary modifications should be made based on a diagnosis.

· Diets that restrict or do not include red meats are best in some cases, and act as insurance in others where definitive diagnosis has not been made.

· Manifestation of one disease can vary from one dog to the next.

· Fish, cheese and yogurt provide good sources of branch chain amino acids.

· Restricting protein can do more harm than good.

· Proteins from sources with high biological value are best.

· Supplemental B vitamins and vitamin E play important roles.

· Never supplement with zinc alone unless directed to do so by a veterinarian.

· Milk thistle and SAMe can play important roles for the compromised liver.

24 *American Journal of Clinical Nutrition* (Nov 2002) Vol. 76, No. 5, 1183S-1187S.

CHAPTER 12
Kidney Disease

KIDNEYS ACT AS A FILTERING SYSTEM by getting rid of toxic waste products. They balance the body's fluid content by reabsorbing immense amounts of water into the blood, produce hormones that help to make red blood cells and help to control blood pressure. The food that your dog eats is broken down and part of this breakdown, along with the normal breakdown of body tissues becomes waste. This waste is sent to the kidneys for removal. When kidney function is compromised, the wastes build up and damage the body.

The filtering units of the kidneys are called nephrons. Kidney disease causes nephrons to lose function, and since kidney damage is progressive and irreversible, nephrons are destroyed if left untreated.

Symptoms
By the time blood test results specific to kidney disease alert us to the problem, about fifty percent of kidney function has been lost[25]. Remarkably, a dog may not show obvious signs of a problem even at this stage. Also, symptoms may not be specific to kidney disease alone. A pet owner may think that increased water consumption is due to weather changes or activity level of their dog. Excessive urination would seem normal given the extra water intake. Lessened appetite may be attributed to any number of diseases or to the dog being finicky. This is especially true when a dog has a history of being a picky eater or is battling a gastrointestinal disease. Although weight loss is another symptom, a dog

---

25 DiBartola, S.P. (2005) Renal Disease: Clinical Approach and Laboratory Evaluation. *Textbook of Veterinary Internal Medicine*, 6th Edition, Vol 2: 1716-1730.

owner may not notice it until the loss is relatively dramatic, or may be pleased to see their heavier-set dog finally losing some weight. Vomiting can happen for any number of reasons and is not uncommon when dogs have a history of eating things other than food, so this symptom may also be ignored unless vomiting occurs frequently. Depression is another sign, but a dog owner may attribute this to life changes within the household or increasing age, or not notice it all if a dog tends to be stoic.

Diagnosing Kidney Disease

The first year of life for small and medium-sized breeds is equivalent to about twenty human years. Each year after that is equivalent to four years. It is prudent to take your dog for a complete physical exam, urinalysis, complete blood count and chemistry panel each year. After all, roughly four years have gone by!

Early diagnosis of kidney disease can have a big impact on quality of life and may also impact longevity. Although early kidney disease can exist even when the rest of the urinalysis results are normal, the concentration or dilution of urine may be a sign that further investigation is required. A urinalysis may also show inflammation or infection, which are both indicators of a need to treat or investigate further.

When kidney disease is present, blood chemistry tests show an elevation in creatinine and urea (abbreviated as BUN for blood urea nitrogen on the test result sheet). An elevation in urea alone does not necessarily indicate kidney disease because urea can increase after a protein-rich meal, is not specific to kidney function alone, and has been known to rise in some raw-fed dogs. A reduction in kidney function can also cause increased potassium, calcium and phosphorus to circulate in the blood. This is why a blood chemistry panel is critical to diagnosis.

The Whole Truth

While kidney disease is often a primary problem, pet owners must be honest with their veterinarians if they hope for a positive outcome. An elevation in urea may lead a veterinarian to wonder about an underlying problem but if feeding raw foods is the cause, the veterinarian needs to know about it. Also, an elevation in creatinine may warrant further investigation despite that some pet owners shrug the elevation off as something to be expected in raw-fed dogs. My client files over the last eight years have consistently shown that no raw-fed dog has had elevated creatinine without also having compromised kidney function.

Causes and Mechanisms

Although dog owners may be anxious to point to one cause of kidney disease, there are many possibilities. Sometimes nothing specific can be determined. The most common causes include ingestion of antifreeze or other poisons, medications given for extended periods of time, excess vitamin D, disease in other organs (i.e., diabetes), chronic kidney infections, genetics, crystallization of excess calcium and aging.

Vitamin D is activated in the kidneys and is required for proper absorption of calcium and phosphorus. Excess vitamin D in combination with excess calcium and phosphorus promotes the formation of crystals in the kidneys. Although calcium oxalate in the kidneys is usually found when it aggregates into a stone, the crystals can start forming in the urine in the kidney area.

There may be a connection between the aging process and some medications that cause kidney disease. An older animal is more likely to develop medical conditions that require certain medications. Some of these medications can damage kidneys. The geriatric animal with declined kidney function has an even tougher battle because drug absorption, distribution and excretion can be altered due to reduced muscle mass and gastrointestinal function.

Dietary Management

There are several important steps that can help impaired kidneys and general body function.

1. Ensure water consumption
2. Reduce dietary phosphorus
3. Avoid plant-based oils
4. Feed fish body oil
5. Ensure sufficient dietary potassium intake
6. Decrease dietary sodium intake
7. Ensure ample vitamin B intake
8. Avoid excess dietary protein

Water

There is a progressive decline in the capacity of impaired kidneys to concentrate urine. When there is not enough water in the body, hormone signaling and blood pressure changes force the kidneys into survival mode, which causes them to conserve water by concentrating urine. If their ability to do this is impaired, they are placed under further stress.

Although we may think of urine as the way the canine body excretes water, output also occurs through respiration, the gastrointestinal tract, entire urinary system and skin. These natural water losses can leave the kidneys in a position to try and concentrate urine.

Fresh foods have high moisture content. In addition, adding a little extra water to the food bowl can be helpful for dogs that rarely drink fresh water. In cases where a dog is feeling too ill to eat, low-salt homemade broths will usually tempt the dog to drink. In some cases, pediatric electrolyte replacement liquids like Pedialyte® can also be helpful.

Dietary Phosphorus

Of all the dietary changes we can make, reducing phosphorus has the greatest impact. In experimental canine models, eating a low-phosphorus diet increased dogs' survival rates by 42% compared to dogs consuming a high-phosphorus diet.[26]

Before the amount of dietary phosphorus can be reduced, we must know how much a diet provides in the first place. The USDA website is a great place to start (http://www.nal.usda.gov/fnic/foodcomp/search).

Be aware that the USDA website lists foods for human consumption. For this reason, the nutrient values do not include bone. As an example, chicken wings are listed, but the nutrient values are for the meat or meat and skin alone.

Create a spreadsheet and enter all foods being fed. Enter the mineral values for these foods in separate columns and add them up so you have a total per mineral. Here is an example of what your spreadsheet might look like.

26 Brown, S. A., Crowell, W. A., Barsanti, J. A., White, J. V., Finco, D. R. (1991) Beneficial effects of dietary mineral restriction in dogs with marked reduction of functional renal mass. *Journal of the American Society of Nephrology, Vol. 1 (10): 1169-1179.*

Example of a Dietary Spreadsheet

	3 oz ground beef, pan browned, 15% fat	2 oz beef heart, simmered	5 oz glutinous white rice, boiled	1 oz raw carrot	Total
Calcium (mg)	19	2.83	2.83	9.36	34.02
Phosphorus (mg)	202	144.02	11.34	9.92	367.28
Magnesium (mg)	21	11.91	7.09	3.40	43.40
Sodium (mg)	76	33.45	7.09	19.56	136.10
Potassium (mg)	346	124.17	14.17	90.72	575.06
Iron (mg)	2.49	3.62	0.20	0.09	6.40
Copper (mg)	0.08	0.32	0.07	0.01	0.48
Zinc (mg)	5.63	1.63	0.58	0.07	7.91
Manganese (mg)	0.01	0.02	0.37	0.04	0.44
Selenium (mcg)	18.40	22.06	7.94	0.03	48.43
Iodine (mcg)	0	0	0	0	0

A healthy dog requires 130 milligrams of calcium and 100 milligrams of phosphorus per kilogram (2.2 pounds) of body weight, to the power of 0.75. Note the ratio of these minerals (1.3:1) but it is safe to use a 2:1 ratio, 3:1 being the maximum. Once you know that calcium is being provided in the correct amount, your goal is to reduce phosphorus only. I start by using 75% of the phosphorus number and will reduce further if needed. This can be accomplished by searching through the USDA website for foods that provide less phosphorus. Keep in mind that changing foods will impact other mineral and vitamin values, as well as calories, protein, fat and carbohydrates.

Note to readers feeding grains: Glutinous (sticky) white rice has lower phosphorus content than other grains.

Note to raw feeders: Reducing RMBs is the easiest way to reduce phosphorus dramatically. This also reduces calcium, but it can be easily increased again by adding eggshell. Pay attention to other mineral values that may be affected by reducing RMBs and change the diet accordingly.

Oils

A 1998 study demonstrated that "the type of dietary fat offered to dogs alters the rate of progression of kidney disease. In particular, fish oil supplementation lowered plasma cholesterol concentrations and slowed the rate of progression of kidney disease. In contrast, vegetable oil was deleterious to kidney function."[27]

Potassium and Sodium

Dogs excrete dietary potassium in their urine and feces. Many dogs with chronic kidney disease experience an increase in urine production resulting in excessive loss of potassium. When kidney function has been compromised, the proportion of potassium loss in feces increases. This means that even a dog that is not urinating excessively can be deficient in potassium.

Hormonal gatekeepers and changes in the way the body handles potassium excretion can make it difficult for blood tests to identify potassium deficiency. The amount of circulating potassium in the blood does not always point to excessive potassium loss. For this reason, a diet for dogs with chronic kidney failure should provide a normal amount of potassium. In cases where a dog is not eating well, an increase of dietary potassium may be required because less food equals smaller amounts of all nutrients being ingested, yet potassium excretion may be increased. This can lead to a weakened state. Some dogs vomit from nausea. These animals will lose some minerals, including potassium, sodium and chloride in the vomitus, which further increases vitamin and mineral loss in kidney disease.

As mentioned in the chapter on heart disease, the hormone aldosterone plays a key role in controlling sodium and potassium status. Sodium increases blood pressure (hypertension), and this increased pressure in the circulation of the kidneys plays a critical role in the progression of kidney disease. Sodium restriction is a vital part of dietary changes.

Fresh foods without added salt still provide sodium. Some foods are better options than others when putting together a relatively low-sodium diet. The USDA website lists the sodium content of foods. It should be used diligently when formulating diets for dogs in chronic kidney failure.

---

27 Brown, S.A., Brown, C., Crowell, W., Barsanti, J., Finco, D.R. (1998) Effects of dietary fatty acid composition on the course of chronic renal disease in dogs. *Journal of Laboratory and Clinical Medicine;* 131: 447-455.

Note to raw feeders: Some RMBs provide more sodium than others. For example, turkey neck and chicken carcass provide much more sodium than is usually best for dogs with kidney disease. Of course, the amount being fed impacts the diet tremendously, but as a general rule, these two RMB sources should be left out of the diet.

Excessive sodium restriction can backfire because the body retaliates by conserving as much sodium as possible, increasing blood pressure and fluid retention. It would be difficult (but not impossible) to reduce sodium to such an extent when feeding a home-prepared diet because foods contain a certain amount of sodium that we cannot remove.

B Vitamins

Even healthy dogs can be deficient in these vitamins when the diet is predominated by ingredients low in B vitamins such as chicken, turkey, cheese or fish, but dogs with kidney disease are at greater risk no matter what they are fed. B vitamins are water-soluble and so are excreted mainly through urine. This excretion accelerates as the dog urinates more frequently and/or a greater volume due to kidney disease. These dogs may also eat less and/or vomit due to nausea. Again, less food ingested means fewer nutrients consumed.

B vitamins play key roles for almost every body function we can imagine, including increasing appetite. This is important in cases of kidney disease. A dog may want to eat less (compromised kidney function can lead to nausea because kidneys that cannot do their jobs well allow circulating waste to build up), and therefore will take in fewer B vitamins which further decreases appetite.

Protein

Dog owners have passionate arguments about protein restriction in cases of kidney disease. Some say we must restrict protein while others insist that this is an outdated idea and that the focus should not be the amount of protein being fed, but its biological value. Certainly, foods with high biological value are good choices for any dog, especially those with compromised kidney or liver function. Biological value is one measure of the quality of the protein in food and is based on how much protein nitrogen the body retains from the total amount provided in the food. The decision to restrict protein or not should be based on an understanding of what happens in the body when kidney disease is present. Increased protein delivery to the kidneys can increase blood pressure in the kidneys and thus increase nephron damage.

Although we seem to have an emotional attachment to feeding dogs large amounts of high quality protein, in reality they do not need very much of it to meet their needs. This is important to consider when we discuss excess protein because the word "excess" can be relative.

A carbon skeleton is the remainder of an amino acid molecule after the amino group has been removed during catabolism, a process involving the breakdown of proteins in the body during normal cell turnover and tissue repair. Carbon skeletons are derived mostly from glucose and other amino acids. While we may think of these carbon skeletons as waste products, the body is actually very picky about what it will release in full. The body is able to use the amino acids from carbon skeletons, and that is part of the reason why animals do not need very large amounts of dietary protein, as long as all essential amino acids are sufficiently provided. This survival process makes sense when we consider that meat eaters in the wild may not have access to prey daily, or even weekly, yet nevertheless manage to live and reproduce.

Since kidneys act as filters and get rid of waste, it stands to reason that compromised kidney function results in more waste circulating in the bloodstream, and accumulating waste products overburden kidneys. Waste products are derived from protein dietary sources.

Dietary proteins with high biological values (eggs, milk, fish and meats, in that order, having the best ranking) leave less waste behind. Still, catabolism continues, and excess dietary protein adds to the waste load. Compromised kidney function leads to greater amount of these nitrogenous wastes circulating in the blood stream, which in turn increases nausea. One goal of dietary management for kidney disease is lessening this load. Early studies in laboratory animals showed rapid improvement when dietary protein was restricted.[28]

The best indication of a need to reduce dietary protein is when concentrations of urea and other nitrogenous substances in the blood show up on test results. At that point, the disease has progressed, and most dogs are feeling so nauseous that they often turn away from their food bowls.

---

28 Hand, M. S., Thatcher, C. D., Remillard, R. L., Roudebush, P. (2000) *Small Animal Clinical Nutrition*, 4th Edition.

Dogs with kidney failure also seem to have altered senses of smell and taste, which can contribute to loss of interest in foods they previously enjoyed eating.

A proactive way to avoid this is to reduce protein. Again, "reduce" is a relative term. We are not aiming to starve the body of protein, but rather to provide a moderate amount in the diet and reduce it as necessary. There is a practical limit to how much protein can be reduced. A dog's body requires one gram of dietary protein per pound of body weight per day or muscle tissue destruction begins.

Reducing phosphorus in the diet can also help dogs with kidney disease. Meats tend to provide the majority of phosphorus in the cooked diets and RMBs provide much of it in raw diets. Reducing both can help kidneys to cope better.

Supplements for Kidney Support

Fish body oils from sources that do not provide a heavy load of PCBs and mercury benefit the kidneys. Like almost everything else in life, too much of a good thing can be a problem. Excessive amounts of fish body oil are suspected to cause blood platelet coagulation problems. Most veterinarians consider 50 milligrams – 100 milligrams per kilogram of body weight to be safe on a daily basis.

When foods in the diet do not provide ample amounts of B vitamins, a supplement is necessary. This is true for all dogs but, given the excess urination that occurs in most cases of kidney disease and the fact that B vitamins are not toxic, it makes good sense to supplement.

A double-blind placebo study in human patients with kidney disease proved that supplemental CoQ10 decreases serum urea and creatinine. An increase in blood antioxidant levels and a significant decrease in indicators of oxidative stress were noted by the study group.[29] Since this study pertains to people, we do not know with certainty that the same would be true for dogs, nor do we know how much would be required to be helpful. Despite this, I have seen positive results from supplementing with 30 milligrams per 9.09 kilograms (20 pounds) of body weight.

29 Singh, R. B., Khanna, H. K., Niaz, M. A. (2000) Randomized, Double-Blind Placebo-Controlled Trial of Coenzyme Q10 in Chronic Renal Failure: Discovery of a New Role. *Journal of Nutritional and Environmental Medicine*; 10 : 281-288.

Weekly, Kidney Friendly Combination Diet

15 ounces whole lamb shoulder without bone

6 ounces lamb shank

12 ounces lamb heart

2 ½ ounces beef liver

3 ounces lamb rib

3 eggs, large

2 eggshells

12 cups glutinous white rice (cooked measure)

3 ounces cauliflower

2 ounces zucchini

16 ounces sweet potato

13,000 milligrams wild salmon oil

25 milligrams vitamin B compound

7 capsules, vitamin E 100 IU

5 capsules, Allergy Research MultiMin™

30 milligrams zinc citrate or gluconate

350 milligrams magnesium

1 ½ teaspoons No-Salt®

½ teaspoon kelp

This combination diet breaks down as 22% of kilocalories from protein, 45% from carbohydrates and 33% from fat, and provides phosphorus at 66% of requirement, sodium at 92% and potassium at 109%. It provides 707 kilocalories per day and should support the weight of a relatively inactive 40-pound dog.

Weekly, Kidney Friendly Cooked Diet

54 ounces chicken dark meat with skin, stewed

8 ounces beef heart

2 ¼ ounces beef liver

16 cups glutinous white rice

32 ounces sweet potato, baked

1 ¾ teaspoons No-Salt®

¼ *teaspoon kelp*
6 capsules, Allergy Research MultiMin™
17,500 milligrams wild salmon oil
8 ¼ teaspoons NOW® Calcium Carbonate Powder
60 milligrams zinc citrate or gluconate
25 milligrams vitamin B compound
7 capsules, vitamin E 200 IU

This cooked diet breaks down as 27% of kilocalories coming from protein, 42% from carbohydrates and 31% from fat, and provides phosphorus at 42% of requirement, sodium at 68% and potassium at 100%. It provides 1,118 kilocalories per day and should support the weight of a moderately active 60-pound dog.

Chapter Summary

- By the time blood test results alert us to kidney disease, 50% of kidney function has been compromised.
- Increase water intake.
- Decrease dietary phosphorus and sodium.
- Supplement the diet with fish body oils rather than plant-based oils.
- Ensure that the diet provides enough B vitamins and potassium.
- Feed protein with high biological value.
- Decrease dietary protein as required.
- CoQ10 has been proven to help lower serum urea and creatinine in human patients.

CHAPTER 13
Urinary Tract Stones

ALEXA SEEMS VERY CONTENT WITH HER LIFE. Her owners adore her, and unlike some of her siblings, she has no performance duties other than to look as cute as possible when meeting strangers. Her best friend is McKenna, a Yorkshire Terrier that lives across the street. At the moment, McKenna's owners are worried because the veterinarian has told them that she has urinary tract stones but nobody knows what kind of stones they are. In fact, the stones cannot be identified unless and until they are surgically removed.

Some breeds, including Yorkshire Terriers, are genetically predisposed to stone formation. Although dietary manipulation can be helpful, genetics tend to be a difficult hurdle to overcome.

Urate Stones

Dogs sometimes develop urate crystals and stones when they have portosystemic liver shunts. This should be investigated, especially in younger dogs, because surgical intervention is often required to treat them. Some dogs, particularly Dalmatians, are predisposed to urate stones. This is because they metabolize substances called purines a bit differently. Purines are found in foods and some foods have a higher purine content than others. The liver is the site where uric acid is converted to allantoin, a product of purine oxidation. Dalmatian liver cells do not make the conversion from uric acid to allantoin as easily as other breeds do. Instead of the liver cells absorbing uric acid, it is excreted through urine. That may not sound so bad, but keep in mind that uric acid is not very water-soluble and can build up to create a stone. Uric acid stones are not always visible on x-ray.

Dietary changes can help to decrease urate stone formation. Water helps to create more dilute urine. Low-purine foods such as eggs and cheese are also helpful. Knowing what *not to do* is equally important. Never add vitamin C to the diet of a stone-forming dog. Do not add brewer's yeast or a supplement that contains it because brewer's yeast is high in purines. The lowest purine foods for dogs eating a home-prepared diet are:

· Proteins: cheese, eggs, soy protein (tofu, powdered or soy milk), yogurt

· Carbohydrates: pasta, potatoes, rice

· Fruits and vegetables: apple, banana, beet root, broccoli, cabbage, carrot, cauliflower, cucumber, green beans, green pepper, kale, lettuce, melon, peach, pear, pineapple, pumpkin, raspberries, zucchini

· The highest amount of purines are found in meats, especially beef, liver, kidneys, heart, game meats, sardines and mackerel. Chicken and turkey contain less, but still provide more than what could be considered best for dogs that tend to form urate stones.

Purine Levels in Foods[30]

Foods with very high purine levels (up to 1,000 mg per 3.5 oz serving)	Anchovies, brains, gravies, kidneys, liver, sardines, sweetbreads
Foods with high and moderately high purine levels (5 – 100 mg per 3.5 oz serving)	Asparagus, bacon, beef, bluefish, bouillon, calf tongue, carp, cauliflower, chicken, chicken soup, codfish, crab, duck, goose, halibut, ham, kidney beans, lamb, lentils, lima beans, lobster, peas, perch, pork, rabbit, salmon, sheep, shellfish, snapper, spinach, tripe, trout, tuna, turkey, veal, venison

Weekly, Combination Diet for Urate Stone Formers

24 raw eggs, large, without shells

32 ounces whole milk ricotta cheese

48 ounces enriched egg noodles (cooked amount)

72 ounces firm tofu

4 cups whole milk yogurt

3 ounces kale, raw

7 bananas, medium size

---

30 Brule, D., Sarwar, G., and Savoie, L. (Jun 1990) Uricogenic potential of selected cooked foods in rats. *Journal of the American College of Nutrition*; 9 (3): 250-254.

1 teaspoon kelp
1 ½ teaspoons No-Salt®
16 teaspoons bone meal
5 capsules, Allergy Research MultiMin™
15 milligrams copper, chelated
17,500 milligrams wild salmon oil
120 milligrams zinc citrate or gluconate
100 milligrams vitamin B compound
800 milligrams magnesium citrate

This combination diet breaks down as 27% kilocalories from protein, 33% from carbohydrates and 40% from fat. It provides 1,143 kilocalories daily and should support the weight of a somewhat active 80-pound dog.

Weekly, Cooked Diet for Urate Stone Formers
112 ounces firm tofu
36 eggs, large, hard-boiled
60 ounces potato, boiled
7 ounces zucchini, boiled
1 apple, raw, medium size
½ cup canned pumpkin
4 leaves, romaine lettuce
100 milligrams vitamin B compound
7 capsules, vitamin E 200 IU
14,000 milligrams wild salmon oil
7 capsules, Allergy Research MultiMin™
¾ teaspoon kelp
19 teaspoons bone meal
700 milligrams magnesium citrate
1 ¼ teaspoons No-Salt®
12 milligrams copper, chelated
100 milligrams zinc citrate or gluconate

This cooked diet breaks down as 30% of kilocalories from protein, 29% from carbohydrates and 41% from fat. It provides 904 kilocalories per day and should support the weight of an inactive 70-pound dog.

Struvite Stones

Struvite (magnesium-ammonium-phosphate) crystals tend to form when urine contains large amounts of phosphate and magnesium. They can also form in alkaline urine in conjunction with a bacterial urinary infection. Many veterinarians consider an antibiotic to be the first step in treating a dog with struvite crystals. Despite best efforts, it is sometimes not possible to culture bacteria in urine. Nevertheless, bacteria is almost always a factor in the development of struvite crystals and stones. In most cases, urine pH has become too alkaline. A urine pH reading of 7 is considered neutral and higher than 7 is alkaline. Struvite crystals may start to form even with neutral pH. Ideally, we aim for urine pH of 6.0 – 6.5 (a lower pH is considered acidic). Because struvite crystals form in alkaline urine in conjunction with a bacterial urinary infection, many veterinarians use antibiotic treatment alone to resolve the struvite crystal problem. If antibiotics fail, dietary manipulation can be helpful.

Lowering dietary phosphorus may be helpful, but do not be too quick to also lower the amount of magnesium unless the diet truly provides too much of it. Magnesium is required to prevent calcium crystallization. The dog requires this mineral, and reducing the amount to less than is required could affect the status of other minerals.

Acidifying Urine

When urine pH is high, most dog owners want to lower it through diet. One of the first things people search for is a list of alkaline and acidic foods. The approach may sound reasonable but goes against the wisdom of the body. The body is able to regulate itself. A food classified as acidic may not remain that way once it enters the body. Consider what happens in the gut after a meal in ingested:

When food comes into the stomach, acid production goes up. However, depending on the composition of the meal, the pH may go up or down transiently. If the meal contained a lot of vegetables or fruit, which has a pH around 2, total stomach pH may go down or stay the same. If it contains a lot of meat or dairy, with a pH around 5 – 6, the pH may briefly increase from about 2 to about 4 or so until the food is all mixed up with acid, and the stomach contents start emptying.

While the gastric pH changes, the bloodstream gets an alkaline flood from the circulation around the stomach. This is the measurable "alkaline tide" that occurs in the bloodstream during a meal. The urinary system helps handle the excess alkali and sends it out through the urine. As a result, urine tends to be less acid around mealtime. More frequent meals lead to less fluctuations in urine acidity.

As in so many cases, the uniqueness of a dog's metabolism plays a role in acidifying urine through diet. Most dogs produce more acidic urine when fed a decreased amount of carbohydrate. We can also reduce urine pH with protein loaded with sulfur-amino acids (muscle meat, eggs) and chloride forms of minerals such as calcium chloride. We can raise urine pH with vegetable proteins (they do not contain much sulfur, so little sulfur acid is excreted in the urine) and carbonate forms of minerals such as calcium carbonate.

Individual metabolism varies. What best applies to one dog may not work in exactly the same way for your dog. Your best bet is to visit the pharmacy or health food store and purchase some pH strips. Catch some of the first urine of the day and test it for a few days in row after changing the diet. Keep a log to see how the diet changes are affecting urine pH.

Urine strips can usually be purchased at pharmacies or swimming pool supply companies. My favorite brand is Chemstrip® 10 SG by Roche Diagnostics. These can be ordered by most pharmacies. I like them because they show urine pH, protein, glucose, ketones, blood, bilirubin, urobilinogen, nitrites, leukocytes and specific gravity. They cost more than regular pH strips but also show a more complete result. While this may not be necessary in some cases, I prefer to see the bigger picture. Being able to see more changes in urine allows you to consult your veterinarian more quickly about possible problems.

False Test Results

In most cases, test results for urine pH are accurate; however, there are two things you should know. Urine pH elevates the longer a urine sample sits around. Also, even if there were no crystals initially present in a sample, they can precipitate out as urine is cooled (when the sample is put into the refrigerator until analyzed or picked up by the lab). High levels of struvite crystals in the urine do not therefore necessary mean that the dog has a problem. Struvite crystals form whether the urine has been sitting around in your home or at the clinic, so it is important that you get a urine sample to your veterinarian right away. One of the key factors in receiving a true result is how quickly the test is performed.

When taking the dog's urine sample to your veterinarian, ensure that you have first been given a proper, sterile container for collection from the clinic. Washed plastic containers from the home can harbor bacteria that could show up in a urine sample. For the most accurate results, the sample should be analyzed when warm and freshly obtained.

Supplements for Struvite Crystal Formers

Vitamin C can help to acidify urine, but I do not like to use it for this reason alone. We have discussed that vitamin C together with urinary loss of calcium can cause calcium oxalate crystals to form. A stone-forming dog can easily go from one kind of crystal formation to another, so supplementing with vitamin C is a big gamble.

Cranberries do not acidify urine, but they have properties that help keep bacteria from adhering to the bladder walls. They can be a good addition to the diet, unless your dog produces stones that have a calcium oxalate core with a struvite shell. Cranberries are high in oxalate. If you are not certain that the dog has a struvite stone without the added complications of oxalate, do not use cranberries in the diet. Wild salmon oil is supportive of kidneys and can be used to help reduce inflammation.

Weekly, Raw Diet for Struvite Stone Formers

23 ounces turkey thigh, with bone

12 ounces turkey wing

24 ounces turkey breast with skin, boneless

7 ounces rabbit

24 ounces beef heart

20 ounces beef kidney

6 ounces beef liver

48 ounces ground beef, 15% fat

1 egg, large with shell

16 ounces whole milk yogurt

36 ounces sweet potato

6 leaves, romaine lettuce

7 bananas, medium size

16 ounces broccoli

7 capsules, vitamin E 200 IU

21,000 milligrams wild salmon oil
1 teaspoon kelp
750 milligrams magnesium citrate
15 milligrams manganese
110 milligrams zinc citrate or gluconate

This raw diet provides 1,411 calories per day that break down as 40% from protein, 18% from carbohydrates and 42% from fat. It should support the weight of a moderately active 100-pound dog.

Weekly, Cooked Diet for Struvite Stone Formers

2 eggs, large, hard-boiled
24 ounces chicken dark meat with skin, stewed
8 ounces chicken gizzards, simmered
7 ounces chicken hearts, simmered
3 cups long grain brown rice (cooked measure)
2 ounces frozen green beans
6 ounces acorn squash, boiled
1 ¼ ounces beef liver, braised
4,500 milligrams wild salmon oil
25 milligrams vitamin B compound
7 capsules, vitamin E 100 IU
¼ teaspoon kelp
7 teaspoons bone meal
1 teaspoon No-Salt®
⅛ teaspoon table salt
250 milligrams magnesium citrate
30 milligrams zinc citrate or gluconate

This cooked diet provides 470 kilocalories that break down as 40% from protein, 20% from carbohydrates and 40% from fat. It should support the weight of a moderately active 20-pound dog.

Calcium Oxalate Stones

These stones occur for two main reasons. The first is genetic disposition. Oxalic acid is a natural part of food, but the way a dog metabolizes it can be due to genetics. Nephrocalcin is a substance in urine that naturally inhibits the formation of calcium oxalate stones, but it is defective in dogs that form these stones. The production of defective nephrocalcin may be a genetic problem. Breeds at high risk include Lhasa Apsos, Miniature Poodles, Yorkshire Terriers, Bichon Frises and Miniature Schnauzers. The second is urinary excretion of calcium and oxalate. This reason may be related to the first because metabolism plays a large role in both.

In addition, although not on the top of the list for causing calcium oxalate stones, certain medications can have this side effect, especially in dogs with a history of being stone formers. For example, furosomide (Lasix®) is a diuretic often used for dogs in heart failure that can cause excess calcium excretion in urine. Cortisone-type drugs such as prednisone can also lead to calcium oxalate trouble.

Diagnosis, Facts and Myths

The only way to know with certainty that a dog's bladder stone is a calcium oxalate stone is to retrieve one and have a laboratory analyze it. No other method can diagnose this stone accurately. Unlike uric acid stones and struvite stones, diet does not dissolve calcium oxalate stones. This is a medical fact. But it seems that for every fact there is at least one myth circulating on the Internet. One such myth is that diet can indeed dissolve calcium oxalate stones. There are directions as to how go about it. To better understand how someone might think that diet can dissolve calcium oxalate stones, we need to discuss this in more detail.

We will use the example of a dog known to have multiple stones. A diagnosis of calcium oxalate stones can only be made after removal and laboratory analysis. There are two options for removal: surgery and flushing out a small stone. I will therefore present a scenario for each option.

In scenario one, all of the stones are removed in surgery and diagnosed as calcium oxalate stones. Later, the dog forms stones again, and the owner assumes these stones are also calcium oxalate. The owner then changes the diet and the stones disappear, leading the owner to believe that calcium oxalate stones can be dissolved through dietary changes. In reality, they were not calcium oxalate stones to begin with.

In scenario two, one stone is passed and diagnosed as calcium oxalate. The owner then assumes that the other stones, still in the bladder, are also calcium oxalate. This may not be the case at all. It is possible for a dog to have more than one type of stone at a time. The owner changes the diet and the stones disappear as in scenario one. These two scenarios clearly demonstrate how easy it is to be misled into believing that diet can dissolve calcium oxalate stones.

Many stones are combinations of struvite and calcium oxalate. In these cases, dietary changes can reduce or eliminate the struvite shell, leaving only a calcium oxalate core. An x-ray will show that the stone has become smaller, but the calcium oxalate core remains and the shrinkage is due to the elimination of the struvite shell.

Some people believe a diet is working when calcium oxalate crystals in urine are gone. While this can indeed be brought about through dietary changes, any calcium oxalate stones still inside the body will remain. Crystals in urine do not necessarily mean stones are present in the bladder and vice versa. More often than not, stone-forming dogs can be stopped from forming crystals through dietary manipulation. The crystals flush out of the body and no further crystals are produced.

Logic tells us that since calcium oxalate stones cannot be identified until they are removed, claims involving miracle diets are simply not factual.

Urine pH

While most dogs with calcium oxalate stones have acidic urine, urinary pH is only one factor that may contribute to the problem. Dogs with low urinary pH, and even those that excrete calcium in urine, may not form stones if dietary magnesium is in sufficient supply. Urine pH is only one consideration when assessing the success of dietary modifications.

Dietary Management for Calcium Oxalate Stone Formers

There are eight steps that we can take to manage this problem.

1. Increase water intake.

2. Choose a calcium source carefully.

3. Reduce dietary sodium.

4. Maintain a normal amount of dietary magnesium but ensure it is not magnesium chloride, which can acidify urine.

5. Feed foods with a low oxalate content.

6. Cook vegetables.

7. Do not feed extra vitamins C and D.

8. Feed foods that contain phytates.

Increase water intake

Calcium oxalate stones form when urine is saturated with calcium and oxalate. The more water your dog drinks, the more dilute urine becomes. If your dog does not drink often, add high quality water to food. Your copper pipes add some copper to the water, and there can be other minerals in it as well. Filtered, reverse osmosis or distilled waters are better than tap water. Although we do not want to overfeed minerals, long-term deficiencies of minerals will only lead to more problems.

Choose a calcium source carefully

Citrate chelates with calcium in urine and keeps it from crystallizing. For this reason, some people think that using calcium citrate in a dog's diet works best in cases of calcium oxalate stones. However, this is not always the case when this scenario is considered in more depth. Although I use citrate forms of some minerals, calcium is not one of them. Calcium citrate is more soluble in urine. Because of this, more of it is excreted in urine, which increases the chances of it binding with oxalate and negates any potential benefits.

Reduce dietary sodium

Sodium excretion amplifies calcium excretion. Less wasted sodium translates to less calcium in the urine and therefore less calcium to connect with oxalate. Choose foods that provide the least amount of sodium possible and do not add salt to the diet. However, maintain a minimum of 75 milligrams of sodium per 1,000 kilocalories fed, or the kidneys begin retaining sodium. It would be very difficult to produce a meat-based diet that did not provide at least this amount.

Maintain a normal amount of dietary magnesium and phosphorus

Magnesium inhibits calcium oxalate stone formation. Magnesium and phosphorus also prevent absorption of excess calcium, so they should be provided in normal amounts. In the case of kidney disease, decrease the amount of dietary phosphorus (keep in mind that stones do not necessarily translate to kidney disease). If we lower the amount of phosphorus by too much, we encourage the body to absorb excess calcium and therefore excrete more as well, which sets up a scenario for more calcium oxalate trouble.

Feed foods with a low oxalate content

Reducing the oxalate content of the diet may be helpful. The following lists[31] of foods provide low oxalate content.

- Dairy: butter, cheese, milk, yogurt
- Fruits: apples (peeled), cantaloupe, cherries, honeydew, mangoes, nectarines, watermelon
- Grains: cornflakes (Kellogg's®), egg noodles, rye bread, white rice, wild rice
- Legumes: lentils
- Meats: beef (do not use organ meats), chicken, eggs, flounder, haddock, lamb, pork, turkey
- Vegetables: acorn squash, cabbage (white), cauliflower, cucumber, green peas, lettuce (iceberg), pepper (red), turnip roots, zucchini
- Cook vegetables. Cooking reduces the oxalate content of foods. Boiling accomplishes this better than does steaming.

Do not feed extra Vitamins C and D

Vitamin C can acidify urine, but it can also bind with calcium in urine and creates oxalate. Vitamin D aids in the absorption of calcium. Your dog continues to need vitamin D just like calcium, but excess vitamin D can force the body to absorb excess calcium. A calcium-oxalate-stone-forming animal will excrete excess calcium in urine, predisposing it to more trouble. Provide vitamin D by exposing your dog to direct sunlight for 30 minutes daily or supplement only to meet minimum requirement.

Feed foods that contain phytates

Phytates are substances found in dietary fiber and can reduce absorption of some minerals. Phytates may be classified as antinutrients for this reason, so we do not want to overfeed them. They can be a part of dietary manipulation to address calcium oxalate problems.

---

31 Low Oxalate Foods (http://www.branwen.com/rowan/oxalate.htm).

Supplements for Calcium Oxalate Stone Formers

Stones can scrape delicate tissues, leaving the dog prone to bleeding in the bladder, and thus susceptible to bacteria that cause urinary tract infections. Medications may be used to address this, and wild salmon oil can reduce inflammation in these areas.

B vitamins are important in all cases of urinary tract stones because they are water soluble and excreted in urine. A deficiency of vitamin B-6 has been associated with calcium oxalate stone formation in cats. Whether or not this is true in dogs remains unknown.

Vitamin E should be a part of all home-prepared diets, especially when dietary fat increases.

Weekly, Combination Diet for Oxalate Stone Formers

7 ounces whole milk yogurt

28 ounces chicken breast with skin, boneless, raw

6 ounces ground beef, raw, 15% fat

6 ounces cauliflower, boiled

1 cup frozen peas

7 ounces acorn squash, boiled

7 cups long grain rice, (cooked measure)

2 capsules, Allergy Research MultiMin™

3 ¼ teaspoons calcium carbonate

40 milligrams magnesium citrate

½ teaspoon No-Salt®

5 milligrams copper, chelated

30 milligrams zinc citrate or gluconate

¼ teaspoon kelp

50 milligrams vitamin B compound

7 capsules, vitamin E 100 IU

5,000 milligrams wild salmon oil

This combination diet provides 506 kilocalories that break down as 28% from protein, 42% from carbohydrates and 30% from fat. It should support the weight of an active 17-pound dog.

Weekly, Cooked Diet for Oxalate Stone Formers

65 ounces chicken dark meat with skin, stewed
32 ounces zucchini, boiled
6 ounces cantaloupe
10 cups white rice (cooked measure)
12 teaspoons bone meal
2 ½ teaspoons calcium carbonate
500 milligrams magnesium citrate
2 teaspoons No-Salt®
10 milligrams copper, chelated
45 milligrams zinc citrate or gluconate
7 capsules, Allergy Research MultiMin™
¾ teaspoon kelp
15,000 milligrams wild salmon oil
100 milligrams vitamin B compound
7 capsules, vitamin E 100 IU

This cooked diet provides 955 kilocalories that break down as 30% from protein, 30% from carbohydrates and 40% from fat. It provides phosphorus at only 82% of the recommended allowance. This is the diet to consider if your moderately active 70-pound dog is in early renal failure and has calcium oxalate crystals.

Chapter Summary

- Increase water consumption in all cases of urinary tract stones.

- Vitamin C can acidify urine.

- Vitamin C and calcium excreted through urine combine to create calcium oxalate.

- Struvite crystals are usually associated with a urinary tract infection. More rarely, calcium oxalate crystals can also be associated with infection.

- Foods classified as acidic or alkaline may not affect urine pH as expected.

- Struvite crystals can form in urine that is left to sit and cool, and its pH will also rise.

- Stones can only be identified as calcium oxalate if removed and analyzed.

- A diet that succeeds in dissolving the struvite shell of a stone with a calcium oxalate core may lead people to believe that diet can dissolve calcium oxalate stones.

- Wild salmon oil and omega-3 oils have anti-inflammatory properties.

CHAPTER 14
Hypothyroidism

N OAH HAS EXPERIENCED CLASSIC SIGNS OF SLUGGISH THYROID for several months. His coat has been shedding excessively, his skin is very flaky and he is spending much of his day sleeping. Although he is being fed much less food, Noah cannot seem to shed his excess weight.

Noah's owner has encountered some financial difficulties and is anxious to save a little money if possible. For this reason, she asks the veterinarian for a less-expensive and commonly-offered testing option called "wellness testing." This includes a test for T4 (thyroxine), the hormone that the thyroid gland produces. The test result shows a normal amount of circulating T4 and Noah's owner is pleased that her dog is not hypothyroid, but wonders what else the problem might be.

Perhaps depression is what is leading Noah to sleep so much. His owner purchases a new toy and takes him for walks in new areas so he can have more excitement in his life. While the dog seems happy with these changes, he is not more active and in fact, sleeps even more of the day away.

The owner brushes Noah vigorously to try to get rid of the dead hair and stop the shedding. This does not have the desired effect. Instead, one month later, it seems the Noah's skin has even more flakes than before.

A source of omega-3 fatty acids is added to the dog's diet to improve skin and coat. Unfortunately, one month later, the dog looks to be in worse condition than ever and has gained yet another pound of body weight. Frustrated, his owner visits the veterinarian one more time.

This time, the veterinarian asks for a full blood chemistry profile and Noah's owner agrees. The results show that while T4 is only very slightly lower than normal, TSH (thyroid stimulating hormone) is very high.

We can spend more money by having to run tests more than once than if we had agreed to run a full chemistry panel from the start. This is especially true in the case of a hypothyroid dog because T4 alone does not tell the whole story. In fact, the TSH test is commonly recommended, but W. Jean Dodds, DVM, states that published research shows poor predictability for primary hypothyroidism in dogs and minimal testing should include T4, free T4 by any validated method, and thyroglobulin autoantibody.

The pituitary gland controls the thyroid gland. The pituitary gland releases TSH, and TSH triggers the thyroid to produce hormones, including T4. The body recognizes when the thyroid gland is being lazy and tries to activate it by releasing more and more TSH. Initially, a dog with hypothyroidism may have normal circulating T4, but this is only because more TSH is being released. Once exhausted, the thyroid gland cannot produce enough T4 even when the pituitary gland demands it. So, by the time T4 is low, the pituitary and thyroid glands have both been overworked. Looking only at T4 may cost less, but it does not show the veterinarian a complete picture and can fail to indicate a thyroid problem. This is why Noah was not properly diagnosed a few months ago.

Management of Hypothyroidism

Once the thyroid gland is exhausted, administration of thyroid replacement must be done daily for the remainder of the dog's life. Dietary measures involve nothing more than ensuring the dog is being fed a balanced diet.

A common question from dog owners is whether or not to continue feeding kelp. The thyroid gland continues to require iodine in order to function, and kelp may continue to be fed. Remember to keep in mind the iodine content of the kelp you purchase.

Dietary calcium can impede the absorption of thyroid medication. This is not a problem in most cases as your veterinarian can run tests to check the dog's thyroid levels and adjust the dose accordingly. In some odd cases, however, when the medication does not seem to be doing a good job, giving the medication away from a calcium-rich meal can make a positive difference.

Chapter Summary

- Normal T4 does not necessarily indicate normal thyroid gland function.

- Elevated TSH points to underactive thyroid function.

- Weight gain, lethargy, excessive shedding and/or flaky skin can be signs of an underactive thyroid.

- Hypothyroidism is managed by administration of medication daily for the lifetime of a dog.

- Dietary changes are not applicable other than to correct any imbalances that might exist.

- Iodine continues to be fed.

- Give thyroid medication at a different time from calcium-rich meals if the thyroid medication does not seem to be having the desired effect.

CHAPTER 15
Pancreatitis

O UR BUNDLE OF ENERGY, BEAMER, managed to dig his way out of the fenced-in yard. While his adventures remain unknown, he returned home looking depressed and has been vomiting frequently. Perhaps he ate something that did not sit well. As the hours go by, Beamer continues to vomit and his stool is sloppy. His owner makes a trip to the veterinarian, who sends a blood sample to the laboratory. The test results show elevated lipase and amylase. Beamer is diagnosed with pancreatitis.

Pancreatitis is the medical term for an inflamed pancreas. Most cases are secondary to another problem such as gastrointestinal, liver, kidney or heart disease. Generalized infections, obesity, breed pre-disposition, cancer and drugs such as prednisone can also be underlying factors. When none of the above are factors, pancreatitis is considered to be the primary problem with an unknown cause.

Some believe that primary cases of pancreatitis involve a disturbance of fat metabolism, although the process is unknown. Hyperlipidemia (excess circulating fat in the bloodstream) may be something that occurs before pancreatitis strikes, but most studies in this regard are based on data derived from humans. Due to the possible link between excess fat in the diet and primary pancreatitis, high-fat diets are often blamed. Many working dogs and sled dogs consume high-fat diets without incident, but they are not genetically predisposed like breeds such as the Miniature Schnauzer, for example. So, is dietary fat really the problem? The truth is that nobody knows the answer.

Veterinarians report that most dogs suffering from an acute attack of pancreatitis ingested a high-fat meal beforehand. Whether this meal came from a garbage raid or the sudden offering of turkey meat with skin and gravy on Thanksgiving, veterinarians see this connection over and over again. I sometimes wonder whether the link is the fat itself, or whether bacteria from garbage can contents or the growing numbers of bacteria in the cooling turkey and gravy, are not part of the problem. Dogs with pancreatitis have bacteria in the pancreas, and bacteria can cross the intestinal wall to enter the pancreas. My theory aside, one thing is known with certainty. A dog with pancreatitis must be fed a low-fat diet.

Reducing the Risk

Reducing the risk of pancreatitis involves maintaining a dog's ideal weight. Obesity is considered a risk factor. A report showed that 43% of dogs with acute pancreatitis were overweight or obese.[32]

Pancreatitis can be secondary to intestinal immune-mediated reactions such as food allergy or inflammatory bowel disease. Suspicion of food allergy can be minimized and the allergy often controlled through an elimination diet (see chapter on food allergies).

The pancreas is a store house for pancreatic enzymes, and foods high in fat and protein trigger the greatest enzyme secretion. While this is normal response to eating a meal, in some dogs the response is excessive and linked to inflammation of the pancreas. Owners feeding more food than necessary, and especially those who feed treats high in protein and fat, should review the dog's diet and make appropriate changes. Baby carrots and green beans make nice low-calorie treats. Reserve protein treats for serious training rather than handing them out continually. In general, treats should provide no more than 10% of the dog's daily calories.

It goes without saying that dietary indiscretions such as garbage can raids are unacceptable, but some dogs are incredibly adept at finding things to eat even during a walk down the street. While most dogs manage to get away with this behavior, those that are not so lucky can suffer a pancreatitis attack. More training or a muzzle may be necessary when as dog seems out of control and eats everything imaginable because pancreatitis can be a life threatening condition.

Be aware of what family members and well-intentioned neighbors and friends feed your dog when you are not there. A shared ham sandwich slathered with mayonnaise or the greasy drippings from a holiday meal have brought more than one dog to the veterinary emergency room.

---

32 Hand, M. S., Thatcher, C. D., Remillard, R. L., Roudebush, P. (2000) *Small Animal Clinical Nutrition*, 4th Edition.

Dietary Management

Chronic pancreatitis can kill the cells in the pancreas that make insulin, thus leading to diabetes (for which obesity is a risk factor).

Once a dog has had an attack of pancreatitis, there is no option but to feed a diet that is very low in fat. In fact, before dogs can tolerate even this, they are likely to require intravenous fluids and antibiotics. The veterinarian will give strict instructions to provide only water in small amounts once the dog is home. The reason for this is simple: the inflamed pancreas cannot tolerate any stimulus. Hydration is critical. A well-hydrated dog experiences better blood flow to the pancreas and faster healing. Dehydration slows healing, so it is important to follow the veterinarian's advice and ensure that the dog gets enough fluids.

The reduction of inflammation is an individual response. Some dogs tend to heal faster than others. Some cases of pancreatitis become chronic, and the dog must consume a low-fat diet for life, while in other cases, the dog may resume a normal diet within a few weeks.

Like all other dogs with pancreatitis, Beamer needs to be fed several very small meals throughout the day. His pancreas will not produce too many enzymes when he eats very small meals, so, he is less likely to vomit. This in turn will cause him to feel better and cause his appetite to improve. In addition, since he is not vomiting, he can maintain normal electrolyte levels and feel better faster.

Since the pancreas is most stimulated to produce enzymes by foods that are high in protein and fat, a diet for pancreatitis needs to be lower in protein and much more restricted in fat than the dog's original diet. This diet would be too low in calories unless they are supplied through additional carbohydrates. The goal is to provide carbohydrates that are easily digested and provide plenty of calories without having to feed the dog a great volume of food.

Raw or Cooked Diet?

Unfortunately, I have had my fair share of experience with clients that had dogs with pancreatitis. I provide diet plans for dogs eating raw diets, cooked diets and combination diets, and as a rule, do not tend to try and sway someone to a certain method of feeding. However, my experience over the years has been that healing is fastest on a cooked diet. Although we can choose raw foods that are lean, we can skim even more fat from the same food if we cook it. While this may seem like a small difference to us, it translates to a very big one for the dog. I strongly urge you to feed a cooked diet to a dog that is recovering from pancreatitis. In most cases, this same dog can eat a raw diet later on but initially, the pancreas needs every bit of help it can get.

As I stated in the chapter on liver disease, I am a realist. I am including a combination diet of raw meat and boiled rice because experience tells me that some people will insist on feeding raw foods. However, I repeat that this may not be the best approach right now.

Weekly, Cooked Diet for Pancreatitis

16 ounces bluefish

2 ⅛ ounces beef liver, braised

21 cups long grains white rice (cooked measure)

3 capsules, Allergy Research MultiMin™

12 teaspoons bone meal

450 milligrams magnesium citrate

1 teaspoon table salt

2 teaspoons No-Salt®

75 milligrams zinc citrate or gluconate

⅓ teaspoon kelp

7 capsules, vitamin E 100 IU

50 milligrams vitamin B compound

This cooked diet provides 735 kilocalories that break down as 18% from protein, 75% from carbohydrates and 7% from fat. It should support the weight of a moderately active 40-pound dog.

Weekly, Combination Diet for Pancreatitis

2 ¼ *ounces beef liver, raw*
11 *ounces turkey neck without skin, raw*
8 *ounces chicken, dark meat without skin or bone, raw*
14 *cups white rice (cooked measure)*
2 *capsules, Allergy Research MultiMin*™
40 *milligrams zinc citrate or gluconate*
¼ *teaspoon kelp*
250 *milligrams magnesium citrate*
1 ½ *teaspoon.; No-Salt®*
25 *milligrams vitamin B compound*
3 *capsules, vitamin E 100 IU*

This combination diet provides 515 kilocalories that break down as 20% from protein, 72% from carbohydrates and 8% from fat. It should support the weight of an inactive 25-pound dog.

Chapter Summary

· Reducing the risk of pancreatitis involves maintaining a dog's ideal weight.

· Pancreatitis can be secondary to intestinal immune-mediated reactions such as food allergy or inflammatory bowel disease.

· Foods high in fat and protein trigger the greatest enzyme secretion.

· Feed a diet that is very low in fat.

· Feed several very small meals throughout the day.

· Feeding a cooked diet rather than a raw diet is very likely to speed up healing time.

CHAPTER 16
Cushing's Syndrome

AFTER AN OUTSTANDING CAREER IN THE SHOW RING, Noah has finally retired. He was neutered, and so his owner thought it was normal for him to have developed a ravenous appetite. After all, he was less active and probably bored. Noah appeared to gain weight and his pot bellied look was unbecoming. No amount of exercise seemed to help. Noah began drinking copious amounts of water and urinating frequently. A visit to the veterinarian and the blood test results that came afterward showed elevated liver enzymes. More testing brought the diagnosis of Cushing's syndrome (hyperadrenocorticism).

Cushing's is the great pretender of diseases/syndromes. While Noah has some typical signs, there can be others. Intense discussion of this syndrome is beyond the scope of this book, but it is important to understand what lies beneath Cushing's. The symptoms are linked to a prolonged exposure (over several months to years) of the body's tissues to high levels of the steroid hormone cortisol. In some cases, this is due to steroid medications such as prednisone being administered for a long period of time. In other cases, the cause is primary; in other words, the body itself has produced an overabundance of cortisol.

From a dietary perspective, it is important to recognize that Cushing's can masquerade as many diseases affecting just about every body part. Although other problems can arise, the biggest concern is that these dogs become more disposed to calcium oxalate stone formation, hypothyroidism, kidney insufficiency, heart problems, compromised liver function and diabetes. In addition, because of a change in the way their bodies metabolize fats, they are at greater risk for pancreatitis.

Perhaps nothing more than Cushing's can drive home the point that every dog is an individual. Some dogs with Cushing's will develop only one or two problems while others will, unfortunately, have many more. There is not a diet for Cushing's specifically. Diet plays a role in helping the body to cope with whatever the dog is dealing with at some point during the Cushing's journey. That said, there are two approaches to planning diets for dogs with Cushing's. We can either wait until another part of the body needs help and change the diet accordingly, or be proactive — and that is my preference.

The goal is to have a diet that supports this changed metabolism. Since we know that many of these dogs develop calcium oxalate stones, I use low oxalate foods, never supplement with vitamin C and ensure the dog is well hydrated. A dog that would not develop these stones in the first place risks nothing by being fed this way. A dog that is prone to develop them is already one step ahead of the pack if such a diet plan is followed.

We can support the liver by feeding high quality proteins. We can support the kidneys by not overloading the amount of dietary protein (although we want enough protein to discourage muscle wasting) and ensuring that phosphorus is not being over supplied. We can use fish body oils because they are kidney friendly.

When working with dogs that have Cushing's, I keep the possibility of pancreatitis in the back of my mind at all times. For this reason, I tend to formulate diets that are lower in fat. Reducing fat may also decrease caloric intake, which is helpful if the dog is sedentary and prone to weight gain, as is typical of a dog with Cushing's syndrome.

Choosing Supplements

Supplements listed in the preceding chapters on diseases can apply to Cushing's as well. The difference is that not all supplements may be as well tolerated, and of course, we do not want to inundate the food bowl with unnecessary items. I suggest keeping it simple. Base your decisions on what issues the dog is dealing with. For instance, added fish body oil is good for the kidneys but inappropriate for a dog that has pancreatitis. I never add vitamin C to the diet for a dog that has Cushing's because these animals are prone to calcium oxalate stones, and excess vitamin C (ascorbate) is excreted into the urine as oxalate, which may add to the risk of developing these stones. You need to be selective and think things through.

When to Change a Diet

It is obvious that I am an avid supporter of home-prepared diets. What may not be as obvious is that I believe in switching to a raw or cooked diet only when the timing is right. What does this mean? For healthy dogs, timing is not a factor. For ill dogs, it can make a big difference. Dogs with Cushing's are placed on medication and revaluated by a veterinarian to see how the medication is affecting them. Changes in diet during this time would be ill-advised because a dog's reaction would be confusing to decipher. Was it due to the medication or due to the diet? Is the dog continuing to show signs of enormous hunger because the medication is not controlling things well, or is the dog simply motivated to eat because he loves the new food? Did the dog stop eating because the dose of medication is too much for him (this would be a crisis to be dealt with immediately) or because he does not like the new food? Has her water consumption declined because the medication is working well, or is it due to a change in diet that provides more moisture?

If your dog is consuming a dry or canned diet, rest assured that you will be able to feed a home-prepared diet soon. But it is important that your first give the medication a chance to work and the veterinarian a chance to understand test results without throwing a dietary curve into the mix.

Popular Myths

While undoubtedly very useful and full of factual information, the Internet, unfortunately, is also rife with myths that are presented as fact. Sometimes, it is difficult to distinguish between the two.

Two of the most persuasive myths that circulate over the Internet, especially on chat groups, regard the feeding of dogs. This extends to dogs with Cushing's syndrome.

Myth #1

Myth #1 is that dogs cannot digest carbohydrates. Two points are made to "prove" that this is so. The first is that dogs do not have a requirement for carbohydrates. The second is that, unlike humans, dogs are said not to have amylase in their saliva. Since amylase is an enzyme that breaks down carbohydrates, this may seem like a reasonable argument. However, we need to explore some facts.

As discussed in a previous chapter, healthy dogs do not have a dietary requirement for carbohydrates. However, proof that they are very capable of digesting carbohydrates is easy to find. The pancreas produces amylase and, in fact, carbohydrate metabolism in dogs has been well studied and documented. Dogs gulp their food rather than chew it well as people do. It would be a waste of creation to have amylase in the saliva of a gulper.

Interestingly, carbohydrates get a bad rap, and the word "carbohydrates" is often used interchangeably with the word "grains." While grains do contain carbohydrates, vegetables do as well. Although it surprises many people, meat can also contain some carbohydrates. For example, raw beef liver includes just under 4% carbohydrates, raw beef heart provides 0.14% carbohydrates, and even some of the RMBs I sent out to be analyzed contained some carbohydrates.

Another indicator that dogs are able to digest carbohydrates is the dogs themselves. The vast majority of dogs eat commercial diets that contain quite a bit of grain or potato. Whether we agree with it or not makes no difference, because the fact remains that generations of dogs have been eating this way. They obviously lived long enough to produce other dogs, and this would not have been the case if they were unable to digest grains.

How does this myth pertain to Cushing's? It extends to a claim that Cushing's can develop due to the stress that the dog's body experiences from consuming carbohydrates. At first glance, we might wonder if this could be true, but it does not take long to see that this is rather silly. After all, if dogs do not digest carbohydrates (grains being the most evil of the lot according to some folks) and the stress of it causes Cushing's, all dogs consuming grains should have Cushing's. But they do not. By the same logic, all dogs that do not consume grains should never have Cushing's. But some do. Wolves have been documented to have Cushing's, and, at the risk of stating the obvious, wolves do not eat grains.

Some of the "information" regarding carbohydrates and grains in particular is nothing more than a theory based on people with gluten intolerance. It is important to keep the obvious in mind. Dogs are a different species. Oddly enough, we seem to remember this when we point to raw diets being species-appropriate, but we seem to forget it when trying to make a point. Be careful what you believe. Look for facts rather than myths. Your dog's health depends on it. Most people would agree that we would not want to overload the diet with grains, but grains neither cause nor aggravate Cushing's.

Myth #2

This myth is a claim that some dogs have "adrenal exhaustion." It is frequently found on the Internet and causes quite a stir. In theory, adrenal exhaustion would entail an inability to produce enough cortisol. Cushing's is caused by an excess of cortisol.

Sometimes, statements that are not based on facts can sound persuasive. This is especially the case when the language used seems to be at a high level that is difficult to understand. For example, I have read that exhausted adrenal glands produce a biologically inactive form of cortisol. The claim here is that some dogs being tested for Cushing's will have inconclusive test results because there is a resistance phase of the stress response or they are beginning to enter into adrenal exhaustion. It is claimed that when adrenal glands cannot produce cortisol, the body produces adrenal estrogen. This depletion of cortisol and elevated levels of adrenal estrogen are said to bind with thyroid hormone and apparently, disrupt the immune system. Immunoglobulin levels, such as IgA and IgM, drop and so infections are common.

This may sound impressive — unless you are a veterinary internal medicine specialist who has studied and understands these processes. David Bruyette, DVM, Dipl. ACVIM, is a highly respected and well recognized authority in this field. In response to the statements above, Dr. Bruyette states:

"Cortisol is cortisol. It is never biologically inactive. If such a disease or syndrome (adrenal exhaustion) did exist, it would be very easy to diagnose with tests such as a CRH stimulation test and endogenous ACTH. Estrogen raises and does not lower thyroid hormone due to changes in thyroid binding proteins. Estrogen does not "bind" thyroid hormone. Immunoglobin levels are not affected and are extremely crude ways to assess immune function. Infections are not common."[33]

Doug Mason, DVM, DVSc, Dipl. ACVIM, another highly respected internal medicine specialist, responded to this second myth by stating:

"Everything is totally wrong. It's all misinformation. I concur with Dr. Bruyette."[34]

---

33 Bruyette, D. S. (2006). Private conversation about his quote on the *CanineCushings-AutoimmuneCare* discussion group website (http://pets.groups.yahoo.com/group/CanineCushings-AutoimmuneCare).
34 Mason, D. (Oct 2006) Small Animal Internal Medicine, Toronto, Ontario, Canada. Private conversation.

Distinguishing Facts from Myths

While we want to make decisions based on facts for any dog, this is never truer than when we are trying to help a sick one. None of us know all there is to know. When we are faced with a sick pet with a condition that we know little about, it stands to reason that panic can set in. This panic is the set up for acceptance of misinformation, especially when it is presented with confidence. But misinformation, whether written or spoken aloud, is still misinformation. The success of your decisions is based on being able to distinguish facts from fiction. I encourage you to speak to your own veterinarian and veterinary specialists before believing everything you hear or read on the Internet.

Raw or Cooked Diet?

Dogs with Cushing's can do well when fed either way. A consideration here is that Cushing's can be viewed as not one disease but a cascade of possibilities. A dog with elevated cortisol has a compromised immune system and is less likely to be able to cope with the natural bacteria found in raw meats and bones. Will s/he become ill? Nobody can say what will happen with a particular dog and that is the point.

Raw diets tend to be either high in fat (a problem for a dog prone to pancreatitis) or high in protein and, accordingly, phosphorus (a problem for dogs with compromised kidney function).

Weekly, Combination Diet for Cushing's Syndrome

13 ounces turkey neck

24 ounces turkey dark meat, with skin (no bone)

2 ounces yogurt, whole milk

2 large eggs without shells

2 ¾ ounces beef liver

12 ounces ground beef, lean (15% fat)

1 small apple with skin

36 ounces acorn squash

8 ounces cauliflower

2 small zucchini

1 ½ cups frozen green peas

7,000 milligrams wild salmon oil

5 cups glutinous white rice (cooked measurement)
4 capsules, Allergy Research MultiMin™
20 milligrams zinc citrate or gluconate
½ teaspoon kelp
12 ½ milligrams B compound vitamin (¼ of a 50 milligram tablet)
7 capsules, vitamin E 100 IU

This combination diet provides 596 kilocalories per day that break down as 32% from protein, 35% from carbohydrates and 33% from fat. It should support the weight of an inactive, 40-pound dog.

Weekly, Cooked Diet for Cushing's Syndrome

6 ounces cod, baked
12 ounces ground beef, 25% fat
5 cups long grain white rice (cooked measurement)
1 ¼ ounces beef liver, braised
8 ounces cauliflower, boiled
8 ounces zucchini, boiled
16 ounces acorn squash, baked
20 ounces chicken breast with skin, stewed
3,500 milligrams wild salmon oil
¼ teaspoon kelp
6 ¼ teaspoons bone meal
2 capsules, Allergy Research MultiMin™
20 milligrams zinc citrate or gluconate
6 ¼ milligrams vitamin B compound (⅛ of a 50 milligram tablet)
3 capsules, vitamin E 100 IU

This cooked diet provides 507 kilocalories that break down as 37% from protein, 35% from carbohydrates and 28% from fat. It should support the weight of a moderately active 20-pound dog.

Chapter Summary

· Canine Cushing's syndrome comes from prolonged exposure of the body's tissues to high levels of the steroid hormone cortisol.

· Dogs with Cushing's are more disposed to calcium oxalate stone formation, hypothyroidism, kidney insufficiency, heart problems, compromised liver function, diabetes and pancreatitis.

· Although there is not one specific diet to address Cushing's, a proactive approach includes feeding less fat and supporting the organs most likely to become compromised.

· Do not change the diet while your veterinarian is monitoring the dog in an effort to adjust medication.

· Grains do not cause Cushing's. They also do not cause a dog with Cushing's to become sicker.

· A dog that has a compromised immune system is less likely to be able to cope with bacteria found in raw meats and bones.

CHAPTER 17
Addison's Disease

ALLY ENJOYS HER DAILY WALK IN THE PARK. She tries to pull her owner in that direction every time they set foot outside. While she enjoys meeting people there, the best part about the park is that she is given the freedom to play with other dogs. Her favorite playmate is a Miniature Poodle named Tuffi. Usually, the greeting between the two dogs is something to see: play bows, sniffs, tail wags and an excited demeanor as if neither can wait to get the play date going. But lately, Tuffi has been acting oddly. She enters the park in a semi-cowering position and seems afraid of the very things she has always enjoyed.

Ally's owner asks Tuffi's owner if her dog is feeling well. Yes, generally she seems to be but apparently, she has become nervous for unknown reasons. Also, although she has always had a healthy digestive tract, she seems sensitive to many foods lately and develops diarrhea. Her owner has made an appointment with the veterinarian.

Tuffi's blood test results show an elevation in circulating potassium and a low sodium level. For definitive diagnosis, the dog is given the ACTH stimulation or response test. This tests the ability of the adrenal glands to produce the corticosteroid hormone cortisol, and Tuffi's is abnormally low this time. She is diagnosed with Addison's disease, otherwise known as hypoadrenocorticism. Miniature Poodles are one of the breeds most susceptible to this problem.

Tuffi's sudden nervousness and digestive upset can be signs of Addison's, but they are not necessarily present. Dogs can have vague symptoms or none at all. Some dogs just seem "off." Other symptoms include pain in the hindquarters, vomiting and diarrhea, muscle weakness, muscle tremors or shivering and depression. Because all of these things can point to so many other problems, the possibility of Addison's is sometimes overlooked when blood potassium and sodium levels are normal.

In Addison's disease, the opposite of Cushing's disease is occurring. In other words, the adrenal glands are not producing enough cortisol. There are three forms of this disease: Primary (Tuffi's diagnosis), secondary and atypical. While it is beyond the scope of this book to discuss the differences, it is important to determine which of the three a dog is dealing with. Atypical Addison's can become primary so the dog requires careful monitoring.

Fear of Prednisone

Most of the clients coming to me with dogs recently diagnosed with Addison's disease are worried because their dogs are taking prednisone and will continue to do so for the rest of their lives. Owners are usually in a panic about this and want to address the situation via diet.

The fact is, the adrenal glands cannot be forced to produce the steroid cortisol, and no diet will help them to do so. Prednisone brings a needed steroid to the body, and most dogs that take it for Addison's have a great quality of life and normal life expectancy. Prednisone is used under medical supervision to give the body back what it needs. It is not used indiscriminately. Controlled Addison's is not a death sentence. Conversely, not controlling it with prednisone can kill the dog.

Dietary Manipulation

Addison's brings three main issues to the table: excessive acidity of body fluids due to accumulation of acids (acidosis), elevated blood potassium and low blood sodium.

In regard to acidosis, although we want to feed an appropriate amount of high quality protein, loading the diet with muscle meat is probably not the best way to go. Muscle meats and eggs provide high amounts of sulfur amino acids.

The body has hormonal regulators that keep circulating sodium and potassium in balance. There is anecdotal evidence that increasing dietary sodium helps dogs with Addison's disease. As always, individual response can differ, so monitor the dog continuously to see if dietary changes help.

Weekly, Raw Diet for Addison's Disease

3 ounces lamb rib

3 ½ ounces chicken back with skin

6 ounces turkey thigh with skin and bone

6 ounces chicken breast with skin, boneless

16 ounces beef heart

2 ounces beef liver

8 ounces yogurt, whole milk

8 ounces ricotta cheese, whole milk

12 ounces mackerel, canned

32 ounces sweet potato

1 large apple with skin

2 medium stalks celery

2 ounces broccoli

1 eggshell

2 capsules, Allergy Research MultiMin™

60 milligrams zinc citrate or gluconate

150 milligrams magnesium citrate

½ teaspoon kelp

12 ½ milligrams vitamin B compound (¼ of a 50 milligram tablet)

This raw diet provides 520 kilocalories per day that break down as 35% from protein, 27% from carbohydrates and 38% from fat. It provides a normal amount of potassium and two and one half times the recommended allowance of sodium. It should support the weight of a relatively inactive 30-pound dog.

Weekly, Cooked Diet for Addison's Disease

20 ounces canned mackerel

16 ounces beef heart

3 ounces beef liver

24 ounces ground beef, 25% fat

7 cups long grain brown rice

44 ounces baked potatoes with skin

16 ounces yogurt, whole milk

16 ounces ricotta cheese, whole milk

16 ounces chicken gizzards

2 teaspoons canola oil

¼ teaspoon kelp

14,000 milligrams wild salmon oil

7 teaspoons bone meal

4 teaspoons NOW® Calcium Carbonate Powder

450 milligrams magnesium citrate

95 milligrams zinc citrate or gluconate

25 milligrams vitamin B compound

1 teaspoon table salt

This cooked diet provides 1,190 kilocalories per day that break down as 36% from protein, 31% from carbohydrates and 33% from fat. It supplies the recommended allowance of potassium and two and one half times the recommended allowance of sodium. It should support the weight of a moderately active 70-pound dog.

Supplements

Addison's disease responds to medication and sometimes to dietary manipulation (as explained above). No supplements directly address this disease. However, supplements are used to balance a good diet.

Chapter Summary

- Dogs with Addison's disease can have vague symptoms or none at all.

- Medication must always be used in cases of Addison's.

- Atypical Addison's can become primary, so the dog requires careful monitoring.

- Feed an appropriate amount of high quality protein without over-loading the diet with muscle meat.

- There is anecdotal evidence that increasing dietary sodium helps dogs with Addison's disease, but since individual response varies, every dog should be monitored by a veterinarian.

- Supplements are used to balance a good diet but they do not directly address Addison's disease.

CHAPTER 18
Allergies

A LEXA HAS ALWAYS SCRATCHED a bit more than the average dog. Over time, the scratching has intensified and she has had several yeast infections in her ears. Lately, she has been nibbling at her legs and paws. Visits to the veterinarian usually end with prescriptions for creams and prednisone. This does help, but once the prescription runs out, Alexa goes back to scratching, licking and chewing.

Frustrated, Alexa's owner combs the Internet and comes across a number of websites and discussion groups that provide misinformation, namely, that the dog is scratching because she has yeast, and the yeast results from feeding foods that are high in "sugar." She is told to remove carbohydrates from the diet, especially grains and sweet vegetables such as carrots and sweet potatoes. Will this help? To understand food allergies and yeast overgrowths, we need to discuss things further.

Defining Allergy
The body attempts to protect itself from substances it perceives as harmful by sending out antibodies. In the case of food allergy, the body is mistaken in its perception of harm. Obviously, food protein in and of itself is not harmful. However, the body can decide that a certain food (or more than one) is a reason to wage war, and it does so with gusto. Special IgE antibodies identify the food every time it is eaten, and histamine and chemicals are released as a direct response.

Like Alexa, most dogs with allergies scratch excessively, chew paws and have yeast overgrowths. Many will have sloppy stool with mucus and/or vomiting as well.

Defining Food Intolerance

A food intolerance is also a physiological response to a food but does not affect the immune system. The immune system does not react by sending out antibodies and, there is no IgE involvement. Lactose intolerance is an example. The body simply lacks the digestive enzyme responsible for breaking down milk sugar (lactase).

Alexa's Owner Does Not Care About Terms

Reality says that, other than clinical curiosity, dog owners just do not care very much about the differences between allergies and intolerances. The dog is suffering, the owner is suffering, and the bank account keeps going down due to all the necessary visits to the veterinarian. Alexa's owner would gladly label the dog's condition as either allergy or intolerance if only someone could help the poor dog!

Diagnosing allergies can be difficult. Some people ask for blood tests that can indicate allergies, but most veterinarians agree that these tests are not helpful. I was one of those people. Many years ago, desperate for answers for our dog Zoey, I insisted on having her tested for food allergies. We would have all been better off had I listened to our veterinarian. The results indicated that Zoey was allergic to turkey, which she was not. They also indicated that she could tolerate several foods that she had a terrible reaction to. Learn from my mistake and skip the food allergy tests. You are better off putting the time and money into an elimination diet. We will discuss how to do this later in this chapter.

Yeast

Some of the following information is in my first book, but, given the explosion of misinformation that has occurred on the Internet, it bears repeating and expanding on.

A very common myth is that when a dog has a yeast overgrowth, s/he is suffering from a systemic yeast infection. This is said to be true even if we see the overgrowth only in the ears. Should an excessive amount of yeast also happen to be between the toes or around the genitals, "proof" of systemic yeast is said to be obvious. Many websites point to Candida and claim that it is responsible for just about every kind of symptom imaginable from liver problems to gastrointestinal trouble, skin eruptions and much, much more. Systemic yeast is said to be inside the body in even greater quantities than what can be seen in say, the ears.

The truth is that while we may think that out bodies live alone, we actually share them with many other things, including yeast. Yeast is a natural resident of the skin. We cannot see it with the naked eye unless it overgrows, but it is there all the time, coexisting happily on skin. The most common form of yeast in dogs is Malassezia, not Candida. Whether it has overgrown in the ears, on the belly or anywhere else on the surface of the dog, we are looking at skin — one organ. This is not a systemic problem. Systemic or heavy ear/skin infection with yeasts and fungus is often associated with immune deficiency syndrome, like AIDS in people, FIV in cats and systemic lupus in dogs, for example. Systemic yeast is so rare that the finding is sometimes added to veterinary journals. Dogs with systemic yeast will not just scratch or bite at themselves; they will be so ill that they require hospitalization and will often not survive, despite medical care, due to serious underlying problems.

Since yeast is not a new invader but rather, a natural resident, questions become apparent. What causes it to overgrow? Why does yeast sometimes calm down to normal numbers when grains or "sweet" vegetables are eliminated?

Yeast overgrows as a secondary response to a problem. The problem may not be diet-related, although it often is. When this is the case, it is because the dog has an allergy or an adverse reaction to a certain food. Proteins in animal products and grains tend to be the greatest offenders. The dog that is allergic to sweet potato will respond well to the elimination of this food, and the yeast overgrowth calms down. Another dog, tolerant of sweet potato but allergic to lamb, will have the same positive results if lamb is eliminated. There is no direct link between carbohydrates and yeast. It is all about removing the offending food regardless of what it may be.

Alexa's owner is removing grains and "sweet" vegetables from the diet because she has read that yeast feeds on glucose, and carbohydrates are converted to glucose. Unfortunately, she has fallen for yet more hype.

Many organisms use simple sugar as fuel. The brain has an absolute requirement for glucose. Without glucose, coma and death will result. To avoid this disaster, nutrient metabolism is such that carbohydrates and proteins can be converted to glucose when needed. Short of starving an animal, the brain will be given glucose whether or not we feed carbohydrates. Since this is the case, yeast will always have access to glucose. Should Alexa's yeast overgrowth calm down with a diet change, it will be because she was reacting to a certain food protein, not to glucose.

Environmental or Food Allergy?

The million dollar question! Some dogs suffer from both environmental and food allergies. There are clues that can help some dog owners, for example, a dog that scratches only during one or two seasons of the year is likely to have environmental allergies. Since the diet was not changing seasonally, food is an unlikely culprit.

The very first step in determining the cause of scratching is to check for fleas. Many people living in colder climates do not consider this possibility if the dog scratches throughout the winter months. Fleas have a life cycle that allows them to infest a home. The adult flea jumps on the dog and lays eggs that can fall off into carpets, wood cracks, fabric — anywhere that is warm. Even a few fleas can lay so many eggs that it takes very little time to have a flea infestation to develop. You may never see a flea on your dog. Flea dirt (excrement) may be seen, but can easily be mistaken for tiny specks of dirt. In the autumn, when dogs tend to get dirty outdoors anyway, it is easy to think that those specks are just dirt from outside. If it is flea dirt, your dog has fleas. If your dog has fleas, eggs will hatch inside your home regardless of the weather outside.

Many dogs develop an allergy to the protein in flea saliva after repeated exposures. Flea bites can itch for about 10 days even if the flea is gone. Scratching intensifies, and some dogs are so allergic that their skin actually bleeds from all the scratching and chewing. Fleas may crawl anywhere on the dog, but seem to like the anal area, tip of the tail, genitals and ear flaps. Look very closely all over the body but pay close attention to these parts. Use a flea comb and ask your veterinarian to check for fleas too. Most veterinarians can find a flea or one drop of flea dirt so quickly that it is a worthwhile visit.

As long as you are at the clinic, ask the veterinarian about mites. It is possible that your dog is scratching for this reason. Skin scrapings may or may not diagnose mites. Sarcoptic mange can be tough to find because the females burrow under the skin. The males "skate" on top the skin and impregnate the females. There are far more females than males, so the male could be on the chest of the dog while the veterinarian takes a scraping from the back of the dog. You can see why these microscopic devils can present a challenge.

Once you know that you have eliminated fleas or mites it is time to clean up the home environment. An allergy to dust mites is common. While there is nothing you can do to eliminate dust completely, the following steps can be helpful:

1. Vacuum as often as possible and discard the bag afterwards.
2. Change the furnace filter every month.
3. Buy a high quality air purifier. Those that attach to the furnace are most expensive but also the best.
4. Do your spring cleaning now, regardless of the month on the calendar. Send drapes out to be cleaned and vacuum them often from now on. Vacuum mattresses and buy mattress protectors so you can wash them weekly along with the bed linens.
5. Get rid of dried flowers (they gather a lot of dust).
6. Walk into every room in your home and look at it with a critical eye. Do you see any areas that are likely to hide dust?
7. Do not smoke in the house. Smoke adds to the dog's airway irritation and distress and makes an allergic issue more uncomfortable.

Once the home is as dust-free as possible, think about other possibilities. Dogs can react adversely to just about anything. Get rid of those scented candles. Stop using air fresheners and/or carpet fresheners. Use a natural laundry soap that does not have an added scent. Be sure that laundry is rinsed properly. Soap residue can make your skin and your dog's skin itchy. Use vinegar and water or baking soda and water to clean your home. Bleach is a wonderful disinfectant. The idea here is to get rid of chemical residues and added scents that may be adding to or causing the dog's problems.

Pollens and dust are the most common environmental allergens. You can reduce dust, but there is no controlling Mother Nature. Can diet help? In a sense, it can!

Thy Cup Overfloweth
There are two things to consider in regard to diet and allergies. The first is that some dogs suffer from both environmental and food allergies. Once we eliminate the foods that cause a reaction, the cup full of allergic reactions is not quite as full and the dog's reactions calm down.

The second is that people can have something called oral allergy syndrome. Although this has not been proven in dogs, I have seen enough success in dogs to say that keeping it in mind can help. Some plant proteins in foods are similar enough to plant pollens that the animal can react to them. The reaction is usually on the face, and is characterized by intense scratching, runny nose or eyes and sneezing. Sometimes, dogs wheeze as if they have asthma.

Oral allergy syndrome connections to keep in mind:

· Allergy to ragweed can mean allergy to melon, banana, pistachio or celery.

· Allergy to birch pollen may mean allergy to hazelnuts, apples, peaches, cherries, kiwi fruit, pears, plums or melon.

· Allergy to grass may also mean allergy to kiwi fruit.

Elimination Diets

Elimination diets are the most effective for identifying food allergies and sensitivities. Be warned: to do an elimination diet correctly is usually a difficult process for soft-hearted dog owners. But take solace in the fact that your dog will remain happy and may feel so much better.

We know that when allergy exists, the body has identified a substance that it reacts to adversely. The immune system has a memory like no other. It will identify and react against a food allergen forever. For this reason, we need to eliminate all foods that the dog has encountered before and replace these with new foods. The first step is to make a list of all foods your dog has eaten over the last 12 months at minimum. This includes the ingredients in treats and any morsel of food you have given him/her. Think hard and do not count on your memory. Write everything down because from this day forward, the list is a prized possession. It will allow you to choose foods without making the mistake of feeding something the dog has consumed before.

This does not work in the case of rescue dogs where feeding history remains unknown. Do your best to find out what the shelter fed, if they happen to know what a previous owner was feeding, and always keep in mind that shelters may feed a variety of foods. The most common ingredients tend to be rice, wheat, corn, chicken, egg, beef (sometimes in the form of bone meal) and lamb. If you do not know the feeding history of your dog, staying away from these foods is probably best.

What to Feed

Since the foods must never have been consumed in the past, you need to find new ones. Consider all of the ingredients that may have had a protein source in it. For instance, when you think "beef" you need to look for the meat, liver, meal, meat by-products and even broth in commercial diets. For this reason, some simple diets and prescription diets contain duck and potato, rabbit and potato, or fish and sweet potato. If these foods are new to your dog, they may be fed but do not be disappointed if they do not work out. While the foods themselves may be new, there may be ingredients present even in small quantities that continue to cause a reaction. I know dogs that do not tolerate one form of calcium but are fine with another. Should the new diet include even this seemingly innocent difference, results can be poor.

The second option is a hydrolyzed diet. This means that the protein molecules have been made so small that the body does not recognize them. It is a nice theory that sometimes works well, but I know of more dogs than I can count that did not tolerate these diets either. Our Zoey was one of them. This suggests that the size of the protein molecule is not the only important factor in allergic response or intolerance reaction.

Since my focus is home-prepared diets, it may come as no surprise that I feel the best option is fresh-food diets. Raw diets have a bit of an advantage here because we can feed meat and bone from the same animal source. For example, whole rabbit, turkey meat and turkey neck, lamb meat and lamb rib, etc. By doing this, we provide calcium and other minerals from one animal source. That said, dogs with sensitive digestive tracts, and especially those that show inflammation by producing mucus-covered or bloody stool, do not always do as well initially on raw diets. Cooked foods work just as well for elimination diets, so the choice is yours to make.

Many of my clients think there are no new foods to feed their dogs. Many have already fed such a diverse diet that there is little left. In cases where the less expensive options of chicken, turkey, beef and pork are gone, we must use more "exotic" meats. You can sometimes find these in specialty stores, but they will be expensive. Your best bet is to find a raw food co-op. People feeding a cooked diet can still purchase meats without bone there. The next option is to do an Internet search. One client found a venison farm only an hour away, another found a good source for goat meat. There are many places that will deliver all kinds of novel meats right to your door. Consider venison, goat, ostrich, emu, buffalo, rabbit, duck or quail (you need a small dog or a large bank account for this one) as a start. Finally, vegetarian diets are an option if you are truly out of meat sources.

If you think you have run out of carbohydrate options, consider buckwheat (not derived from wheat), quinoa, amaranth, millet, tapioca, potato or sweet potato. All are gluten-free and this may be important since some dogs react to gluten (a protein found in some grains).

Choose one meat source and one carbohydrate source, and then feed this combination for eight weeks at minimum.

Reality Check

An elimination diet begins as an eight-week process. Supplements are added after this time frame. If the diet is successful, you will be feeding the new diet for a long time. You must have easy access to the foods, and they must be affordable. Will you always have access to the new foods even if your dog will need to eat them for the rest of his life? Is there a secondary source for this food in the event that the original source is short of supplies? Are the foods seasonal or available year round?

Starting an Elimination Diet

Alexa's owner is better informed than she was just a short while ago. She understands that there is not a direct connection between glucose and a yeast overgrowth, so she is ready to start an elimination diet. Her bankbook is happy that Alexa has not eaten many different foods, because this allows her to shop at the grocery store. She decides to try beef as the protein and sweet potatoes for carbohydrates. The beef is lean. This is important because most dogs with sloppy stool cannot tolerate a lot of dietary fat. Intestinal food allergy usually includes a strong inflammatory component, and that inflammation can impair fat digestion and absorption. Should Alexa be fed a food with high fat content and develop diarrhea, her owner would wonder whether the dog was reacting to the beef itself or to the fat. Stick with low-fat, especially at the start of an elimination diet trial period.

Once the body has an allergic reaction, it can take several weeks for things to calm down. Despite that offending foods are not being fed, the body needs time to realize that it need not continue over-reacting. For this reason, elimination diets must be fed for a minimum of eight weeks. Do not move forward with a diet until the full eight weeks have passed. During this time, the dog cannot be fed anything but the two items you have selected. This creates a problem for the dog owner rather than the dog, because most owners feel they are depriving their pet. In reality, they are providing relief from inflammation and itching.

The success of elimination diets is directly proportional to owner compliance. If the dog is fed even a morsel of food that is different from his diet, we need to start over with other new ingredients.

Alexa's owner finds this very frustrating. The dog wants treats. Surely one bite of something cannot be all that bad? Wrong. Think about giving a person who is allergic to peanuts just one peanut and you can understand how important it is to stick to the plan. Alexa can be fed bites of her food as treats. Meats can be dehydrated in the oven if a dog likes something crunchy or chewy. Sweet potatoes can be thinly sliced and dehydrated as well. A dog that is eating pasta as a carbohydrate source is eating wheat. In this case, combining wheat flour with meat and water to create a dough to be baked into cookies would be fine. There are ways to provide treats during an elimination diet without messing up the process. Alexa's owner just needs to think out of the box and be creative.

Eight weeks have gone by, Alexa has consumed nothing but the two foods in her diet and she seems to be feeling much better. However, the diet lacks both calcium and phosphorus. Alexa is eating beef, so we can add bone meal to her food. If she was consuming another meat source, we could add di-calcium phosphate to provide these minerals. If the diet provided enough phosphorus, we would add only calcium (calcium carbonate, calcium citrate or calcium lactate). Some dogs react adversely to one form and not another, so do not panic if this happens to your dog. Simply try another form but remember to look at your dog's calcium requirement, because different forms provide different amounts of calcium. A general rule of thumb is to try one new supplement per week.

One week later, supplement the diet with a multivitamin-mineral complex or, at the very least, a multi-mineral. The products made for dogs provide tiny amounts of vitamin and minerals. They are meant to be used in addition to kibble (although this is not necessary to begin with). Multivitamins and minerals made for human consumption are much better suited to meet the needs of most dogs eating a home-prepared diet.

A dog can have a negative reaction to just about anything, and that includes supplements. Alexa's owner will give the dog one capsule tucked inside a hand-held piece of food. This ensures that it is being consumed in its entirety and does not risk the taste of the food changing. For our purposes, the introduction of this supplement is being called day one.

She does not give this supplement the following day. Instead, she keeps a close eye on the dog and stool. As long as everything seems fine, Alexa is given another multi on day three. If all is well, on day four, the dog is given the multi again. The owner watches the dog closely this week. Since all seems well, the next supplement is introduced.

Despite feeding beef, Alexa's diet is low in vitamins B1 and B2. The B vitamin group works as a team. It is better to feed them as a full supplement rather than adding specific ones. Alexa weighs forty pounds and will receive 12.5 milligrams of a multi B compound. These compounds are commonly found in drugstores and health food stores in 25 milligrams or 50 milligram strengths. Her owner simply needs to cut a tablet into halves or quarters. No brand of B vitamins tastes good, and when fed on an empty stomach, they can cause nausea. Alexa's supplement is placed in a hand-held piece of food and fed as a treat. This addition of B vitamins may not be required if your dog is receiving a multivitamin.

If you are feeding sweet potato, vitamin A is usually in ample supply. Dogs convert carotenes to vitamin A. In cases where the diet falls short of vitamin A, a multivitamin usually takes care of the problem. A multivitamin may also provide vitamins D and E, but some do not include vitamin D. In this case, a dog can be fed cod liver oil. It should be introduced slowly. Also keep in mind the vitamin A content as cod liver oil provides large amounts of it. People feeding chicken to their dogs can add vitamin D by feeding chicken skin. It provides 900 IU/100g.[35]

Unless the main protein source of a diet is fish, the diet will need supplementation of omega-3 fatty acids. I suggest adding this last because it brings two possibilities to the table. The first is the addition of another protein that a dog can react to. The second is that added fat may not be tolerated if a dog has gastrointestinal problems. Happily, most dogs do well with wild salmon oil. For those that do not, flaxseed oil can be beneficial. I have better luck with wild salmon oil.

The Devil Within

People are complicated animals and sometimes, we just cannot seem to stop ourselves from listening to the little voice inside our heads that urges us to feed a dog a variety of foods. I am guilty of this myself, and Alexa's owner is not much different. She is a member of a few discussion groups

---

35 Combs, G.F. (1998). *The Vitamins: Fundamental Aspects in Nutrition and Health,* 2nd Edition, Academic Press, San Diego, CA.

on the Internet and continues to read about the many foods that many dogs can eat. Poor Alexa, she thinks. Her diet is so limited. Yes, it is balanced and meets all her needs, but she has been doing so well and things have probably changed. I bet she can handle different foods now. Nervous but happy to be offering her dog something delicious (beef and sweet potato would make any dog happy but Alexa's owner has forgotten that), she gives Alexa a lamb rib to enjoy. The crunching sound makes Alexa's owner very happy and the dog seems to be fine the next day. See? Things have changed! Over the course of the next three weeks, the dog is not only enjoying lamb ribs, but fruit treats, turkey wings, pork heart…and then it happens. Alexa begins to scratch like never before. Maybe things have not changed after all.

Do not follow this dog owner's lead. Your allergy-prone dog has been trying to tell you something you may not want to hear. She or he is a sensitive little being with every right to a long and happy life that does not include mutilating herself and/or having loose stool all the time. Alexa's owner is left in the unenviable position of having to start the elimination diet process all over again. There is a possibility that the dog developed a reaction to beef or sweet potato, so those two foods are now off the list.

The Challenge
Once the elimination diet has been completed, it is possible to challenge the result and begin to feed some of the foods the dog consumed previously. In the example of beef and sweet potato having been the foods fed during the elimination diet, we could remove beef and use chicken. If the dog reacts badly to chicken, we go back to beef and continue this back and forth scenario with other meat sources until we have a clear picture. I do not like this trial and error method because it is at the expense of the dog. Inflammation in the gut makes it more permeable. Once you use a previously fed item in lieu of the new one that has been working well for the dog, you risk another allergic response, which means there is going to be inflammation. With increased permeability, large protein molecules can seep through, and that includes those from the new food that has been working out well. The end result can be a dog that develops an allergy to the new food, and you have to start all over again. Why put a dog through that when you have a current diet that works? The only time I encourage this method is when a client has used almost every meat source available and the elimination diet consisted of something outrageously expensive.

Rotating Foods

There is a theory that says it is best to rotate foods, never repeating a food for four days in order to avoid an allergic response. The idea behind this theory is that the dog is not exposed to the allergen for a long enough period of time to have an adverse reaction. As we have discussed earlier in this chapter, the immune system has a very long memory and will not be fooled this easily. If a true allergy exists, it will not go away simply because a food is fed less often. The body will react every time it encounters this food.

Chapter Summary

· A food allergy is an immune response.

· Food intolerance is a physiological response that does not affect the immune system.

· The brain has an absolute requirement for glucose.

· There is no direct connection between dietary carbohydrates and yeast overgrowth.

· Have your dog checked for fleas and mites.

· Reduce the possible environmental allergens in the home.

· Elimination diets are best for resolution of food allergy symptoms.

· Be sure that your chosen novel protein and carbohydrate sources are affordable and accessible throughout the year.

· Feed one novel protein and one novel carbohydrate for eight weeks.

· Introduce supplements, one at a time, only after you are certain that the foods are tolerated well.

· Food treats must contain only the two novel foods being fed during the elimination diet.

CHAPTER 19
Gastrointestinal Diseases

THIS CHAPTER COULD BE A BOOK UNTO ITSELF. Puppies and adult dogs can suffer from a variety of gastrointestinal (GI) problems, but from a dietary perspective, most are dealt with in the same fashion.

Many dogs are diagnosed with IBD (inflammatory bowel disease) or colitis. IBD is a very general term. It is often used when a stool sample comes back from the lab as negative for parasites in conjunction with a history of intermittent diarrhea, cow pie-type stool and, especially, mucus in the stool. Without performing an endoscopic examination, the veterinarian is left to label this as something, and so the general term of IBD is often used.

The term "colitis" is sometimes used when fecal tests are negative for parasites and the dog's history is as above but includes either fresh blood or mucus in the stool. It may be said that the dog is prone to colitis "attacks," although this cannot be a definitive diagnosis either unless an endoscopic exam has been performed.

Irritable Bowel Syndrome (IBS) is different from IBD. The volume of stool tends to be small, but it is often watery and contains mucus. The dog may have gas and abdominal pain. Bloody diarrhea is rare.

Fresh blood in the stool looks the way you would expect — bright red, liquid blood. The bleeding is likely happening in the lower portion of the bowel.

Black stool, usually rather smelly and tarry looking, also contains blood. The blood originated from bleeding higher up in the intestinal tract (stomach, small intestine) and has been exposed to acid and enzymes.

There are other GI diseases that we could discuss in detail, including more complicated ones like protein losing enteropathy (PLE) where the body's protein is lost through the intestine, but the bottom line is that diets for most gastrointestinal diseases are very similar.

Agreeing to Have Your Dog Scoped

I work with many cases of gastrointestinal disease. They make up a large part of my client base, and most people ask me questions like "Would you agree to have your own dog scoped?"

I never want to play armchair veterinarian. The only thing I can say is that I did have my own dog scoped — twice. A definitive diagnosis can only be made by looking at the intestinal tract and, unfortunately, dogs do not come with zippers down their bellies. Once the veterinarian has ruled out obvious causes for the problem (parasites, ingestion of a foreign item), s/he must know what the dog is dealing with. Does this change how the veterinarian will treat? In some cases it will not, because most of the time, medication to reduce inflammation is the first step. In other cases, the result of the procedure changes everything. For example, ruling out cancer or knowing if the gastrointestinal tract is in trouble at only a certain spot or throughout, can mean the difference between guessing about appropriate medication or getting it right the first time. It also gives the veterinarian an opportunity to find "surprises" that can affect treatment. Here are two examples, one of which includes my own dog.

1. A client with a dog that repeatedly tested negative for parasites decided to have her dog scoped when the animal did not respond to medication or dietary changes. The finding was a nest of worms living happily inside this dog's gut. With proper medication, the worms were expelled and the former diagnosis of IBD became history. The end result was a dog that could eat many different foods, stopped having diarrhea and vomiting and finally returned to a healthy weight.

2. Our own dog, Zoey, was diagnosed with eosinophilic colitis and gastroenteritis after being scoped when she was quite young. Her disease was managed by dietary manipulation. She had not taken medication in years. Suddenly, she had what seemed to be a flare-up: urgent stool covered in mucus and quick weight loss. Neither a change in diet nor the prescribed prednisone helped. If anything, stool production intensified. Within a few weeks she lost four of her

twenty pounds and although she acted happy and seemed to have a normal amount of energy, she was delivering copious of amounts of mucus every few hours.

We saw an internal medicine specialist, who suggested that the dog have a scoping procedure. Since dogs with gastrointestinal disease can tend toward cancer, it was important that this be ruled out. Happily, Zoey did not have cancer. In fact, her gastrointestinal tract looked better than it had when she was first diagnosed, some five years earlier. The cause of her current upset was a bacterial overgrowth (Clostridium perfringens). Two weeks of amoxicillin had things under control. In the spring of every year that followed, Zoey would have the same flare up again. She was treated with amoxicillin for one week at those times and everything went back to normal.

Risk Factors

Despite intensive study, there is not enough known about the root cause of most gastrointestinal diseases. Although there seems to be a connection between IBD and small intestinal bacterial overgrowth (SIBO), nobody can say with certainty which one came first. It is a chicken-and-egg scenario. Did the compromised gastrointestinal tract set up the dog for the overgrowth of resident bacteria, or was the overgrowth responsible for the compromise in the first place? For that matter, some veterinarians do not agree that SIBO exists because the bacteria is a natural resident of the gut.

What is recognized is that that IBD has been diagnosed in puppies as young as less than six months of age and in adult dogs. There is a genetic component, and although any dog can fall victim to a variety of gastrointestinal diseases, certain breeds tend toward particular ones. The German Shepherd Dog, Soft Coated Wheaten Terrier, Rottweiler, Chinese Shar-Pei, Irish Setter, French Bulldog, Boxer and Basenji are examples.

Most cases of gastrointestinal disease involve mucosal inflammation. This disrupts normal absorption of some nutrients and can change normal motility, leading to a change in stool quality and possible weight loss.

Dogs with gastrointestinal disease are also more prone to pancreatitis, but even when this never becomes an issue, malabsorption of nutrients can leave animals weakened and set them up for a series of other health problems. The immune system is involved in most GI disease.

Goals

From a more scientific perspective, the goals of diets for a variety of gastrointestinal diseases may be different. For instance, in protein losing enteropathy (PLE), we want to decrease the protein loss originating in the intestine. In this case, an increase in quality and quantity of dietary protein is important since less than normal is being absorbed and much is lost via the bowel. IBD may or may not involve this problem. From the pet owner's perspective, feeding guidelines are pretty much the same, and the goal, of course, is to stop weight loss, diarrhea and vomiting. For most pet owners, reducing or eliminating medication(s) is also an important goal.

Dogs with PLE take prednisone at minimum and most of my clients want the prednisone gone at all costs. The reality of this disease is that while the odd dog may indeed be able to stop taking this medication, most will not. Before we can try to successfully manage this disease through diet, the dog owner has to accept that weaning away from prednisone must be done under veterinary supervision at a very slow pace.

Dogs with IBD or colitis may also be taking prednisone and/or other medications. In some cases it will be for life, in others medications may be eliminated over time. Others will be able to reduce the amount of medication. Although we can pack gastrointestinal diseases into nice little paragraphs to describe the process and pathways of diseases, dogs can be quite unique in their response to treatment and dietary changes. It is important that dog owners accept the slow process of controlling intestinal syndromes and understand that results can differ from one dog to the next.

Fat

The key factor in dietary management of GI diseases that include loose stool/malabsorption is the fat content of the diet. IBS is the exception to this rule, although I know of dogs with IBS that also benefited from decreasing dietary fat. IBD, colitis, PLE and other diseases of the GI tract require a lower fat diet. The question then becomes "How low is low?"

There is not one answer to this question because tolerance levels vary. Dogs with PLE tend to need lower fat diets than in other cases of gastrointestinal disease. My diets for PLE generally provide about 12% of kilocalories from fat. The very tough cases may include even less fat. My diets for IBD or colitis start with 15% of kilocalories from fat and increase as the dog shows tolerance. In some cases, one of my own dogs being an example, dogs can eat a diet that provides 30% of kilocalories from fat and continue to do well. Once intestinal inflammation is controlled, tolerance to fat in the diet may increase since digestion and absorption are less impaired.

Novel Foods

While fat content is key, there are other important considerations as well. We discussed novel foods in the chapter about allergies. The need for novel foods is also a part of most gastrointestinal cases. Whether this is related to food allergy or sensitivity, the fact is that every one of the dogs I have worked with over the years improved once they were fed foods they had never consumed before. The most important of these new foods is the protein source. Given the option of changing protein or carbohydrates in the diet, protein wins hands down. Of course, changing both is even better.

Gut permeability is an important part of most GI diseases. Intestinal disease usually includes inflammation, and inflammation can greatly increase permeability. Large protein molecules are able to seep through a compromised mucosal barrier. As a result, food allergies are very likely to occur. For this reason, there is a good chance that a dog with GI disease has developed at least one food allergy or intolerance. Feeding novel foods is an excellent way to start the healing process.

Remember to choose lean foods. Lamb may be new to your dog, but it is fatty and highly unlikely to be tolerated well. Better choices are skinless chicken or turkey, venison, buffalo, ostrich, lean fish or egg whites.

Protein

The quality and amount of protein are also important. Most dogs with GI diseases lose muscle mass, and they need protein to repair and build tissues. PLE requires that we feed much more protein than in cases of IBD or colitis. Proteins with high biological values are best, and digestibility is key. Whole egg provides the highest biological value but the yolk contains a large amount of fat. Combining whole egg with extra egg whites works well in many cases. Milk and cheese are second to egg on the biological value scale, fish is third and meat is fourth.

Fiber

Most GI problems are responsive to dietary fiber. The correct amount of fiber and even the type of fiber that will work best is documented; however, my reality in working with dogs is that response is very individual.

Soluble fiber attracts water during digestion and serves to bulk the stool. Soluble fiber is fermented by gut bacteria into short-chain fatty acids, which help both the bacteria and the host. The bacteria that use short-chain fatty acids for fuel are usually the "good" bacteria that do not cause disease in the gut. The host uses the propionate to make blood glucose (back at the liver) and the butyrate and acetate to fuel the gut lining cells (mucosal cells). These cells are far enough away from the gut blood supply that they get their nutrition from the material in the food and from what the bacteria supply as well. So, by feeding soluble, fermentable fiber, digestion is aided, growth of good bacteria is encouraged and health of the mucosal cells is supported. Psyllium and pectin in fruits and pumpkin fiber are in this category.

Soluble fiber may help some dogs to have bulkier stool, but I know of dogs that also reacted by having larger amounts of poor quality stool instead.

Insoluble fiber does not dissolve in water. Flaxseeds, potatoes, skins of fruits and vegetables, and whole grains are common sources. Insoluble fiber is said to be contraindicated in cases of diarrhea because we want foods to absorb water. Here again, my experience differs. I have used cooked potatoes with success many times.

Pumpkin is sometimes touted as a miracle food for firming stool. The truth is that it can work both ways, firming for some dogs and causing diarrhea in others. There is nothing magical about pumpkin. It is all about the type of fiber that works best for a certain dog.

Water

Dogs that experience diarrhea and vomiting are at greater risk of dehydration. Electrolytes (sodium, potassium and chloride) levels can decrease, which leaves the dog feeling and acting very weak. Some dogs refuse food and even water when they feel nauseous. Fresh foods contain about 70% water, but this is a moot point if the dog is not eating. We can usually tempt a dog to drink with meat-based broths. These must be very low in fat. I have used the following recipe successfully:

Broth For An Inappetent Dog

1 *chicken breast, skinless, boneless*
4 *cups water*
½ *teaspoon table salt*
½ *teaspoon No-Salt®*

Preparation: Bring water to a boil. Add chicken breast. Simmer until meat is cooked. Remove meat. Add salt and No-Salt®. Bring water to a boil again. Cool both and place in the refrigerator overnight. Skim all visible fat. Warm this broth to room temperature before offering it to the dog. Pour unused broth in containers in the freezer for future use.

Vitamins and Minerals

Diarrhea and/or vomiting can lead to a great loss of water-soluble vitamins. B vitamins, especially thiamin, are important for appetite stimulation. However, feeding B vitamins on an empty stomach can cause nausea. If your dog will not eat, try adding a liquid form of B vitamins (usually available as baby vitamin drops) to water or broth.

Vitamin C can irritate the stomach and causes diarrhea if overfed. For these reasons, I never use vitamin C in diets that are meant to address gastrointestinal diseases.

Once a dog is eating a suitable, balanced diet, mineral depletion may not seem likely. But consider that the status of zinc is dependant primarily on the small intestine uptake. Dogs with a GI disease that affects the small intestine may also become deficient in zinc. This is usually displayed as poor skin condition and should be addressed if symptoms appear. Do not assume a zinc deficiency because an excessive amount of zinc affects the uptake of other minerals from the diet and thus cause other imbalances.

Secondary hypoparathyroidism (low blood calcium) has been described in dogs with PLE that have a severe magnesium deficiency. In this case, magnesium can be depleted by loss through the GI tract or a dietary deficiency. This affects parathyroid hormone (PTH) because a depletion of magnesium causes body tissues to become insensitive to PTH and decreases its production. In turn, blood calcium drops. Since calcium is responsible not only for bone and tooth health but also for muscle contraction, it is not uncommon to see a dog shaking when blood calcium is low.

Raw vs. Cooked

Due to a compromised mucosal barrier and immune system together with a disposition to bacterial overgrowths, I do not recommend raw diets for dogs with GI diseases. Some dogs with a variety of gastrointestinal problems do quite well when eating raw diets. In fact, some do best when fed that way, but it is out of my comfort zone. The fact is that we cannot know which dogs will do well and which will become gravely ill until we try feeding a raw diet, and that is too big a risk for me to take. Sometimes I start with a cooked diet and wean towards raw if that is the client's preference, but only if the dog proves that s/he is doing better and we can take things slowly. I encourage clients to test the waters. Feed medium-rare meats, and if that seems to agree with the dog, move to rare meats. Think hard about what can happen to a compromised gut if there is a large bacterial load in a piece of raw meat, and if you still want to go there, do it slowly by feeding one raw meal a few times per week before moving forward. Only when the dog has been doing well for several months would I agree to feed raw meats to these dogs, and truthfully, even then, I consider it to be a risk that is not worth taking.

Supplements

One of the challenges of feeding dogs with GI diseases and food sensitivities is that the very supplements that might help them are not always tolerated. For instance, glutamine is required for the maintenance of the gut mucosal lining, but glutamine supplements are usually derived from protein sources or wheat. Should the protein source be one that the dog reacts to, we defeat the purpose. Glutamine is found in muscle meats, so although a supplement may be beneficial to some dogs, I tend to use muscle meats as part of the diet and skip the supplement altogether.

Of the possibilities that insufficient B vitamins can present, weight loss, dehydration, ulceration of mucus membranes, diarrhea and gastritis are at the top of the list for dogs with GI problems. Supplemental B vitamins should be given with food, tucked in a hand-held treat. Although many people think that feeding red meat provides sufficient B vitamins, this is not always the case. Not only do many red-meat based diets for healthy dogs lack vitamins B1 (thiamin) and B2 (riboflavin) but, when we feed dogs with GI diseases, we usually feed less meat. This results in a greater risk of a vitamin B deficiency.

Omega-3 fatty acids are reported to be beneficial in combating inflammation. However, they add fat to the diet that a dog may not tolerate. For this reason, I introduce fish body oil or flaxseed oil to a diet last, when the dog has been stable for quite awhile.

Medium-chain triglycerides (MCT) have a different metabolic pathway than fats normally derived form the diet. They can be helpful due to this difference, but they come with two potential problems. The first is that MCT is found in coconut oil and some dogs simply refuse to eat food that contains this. The second is that, despite the scientific explanations of why it is supposed to work in cases of gastrointestinal diseases, many dogs do not tolerate it anyway.

The positive for dogs that do tolerate is that, like any other form of fat, they add calories, which allows the dog to eat less food and so to digest less while maintaining a healthy weight. Because of the negative relationship between dietary fat and most GI diseases, I do not attempt to add any supplemental fat in any form until the dog is doing very well for at least three months.

Probiotics are healthy bacteria normally found in the gut. Supplementation with probiotics can cause viable organisms to flourish in the intestinal tract. Note that I mentioned viable organisms. It does little good to feed probiotics that are not viable, yet some products provide just that. You can get proof that a product is viable by asking the supplier for a laboratory assay, also known as a certificate of analysis.

Acidophilus is the best-studied probiotic in dogs. Others may also be helpful, but for my money, I want something that is known to work. Even something as healthy as acidophilus can cause a negative reaction in a very sensitive dog. I choose to add this supplement only after novel foods have been introduced.

Digestive enzymes can help some dogs, but most products include a protease (the enzyme that helps to break down protein) from an animal source. If you are feeding pork as a novel protein and the protease happens to be derived from pork, this does not present a problem; but if it introduces a new protein, you risk a reaction. Ask about the source of the protease in your chosen product. If it is not suitable, opt for plant-based enzymes instead. A dog can react to these as well, but the risk is less.

Sample Plan

Having experienced GI disease in our Zoey, I wish that I could give you a sample diet to try. I know first hand how frustrating and scary these issues can be, and if you are anything like me, you want a quick fix. As described above, the first step is to find novel foods. Since I cannot know which foods would be new to your particular dog, the best I can offer is a step-by-step guideline that works in most cases.

To do this, I will use buffalo and buckwheat as example novel foods, but remember that I do not favor these foods in particular. Rather, they are being used to show you the process of implementing a diet plan with your selected foods. You can follow the steps with the aid of your spreadsheet, so that you know which supplements may be necessary.

Both foods are noted as cooked weights/amounts; in other words, how much each should weigh or measure after they have been cooked.

One and one half cups of boiled buckwheat together with three ounces of roasted buffalo meat provides 343 calories. This should support the daily caloric need of a moderately active 12-pound dog. Add $\frac{1}{16}$ teaspoon table salt and $\frac{1}{16}$ teaspoon No-Salt® to provide, sodium, chloride, potassium and a little iodine.

Once these foods and supplements are mixed together, wean the dog away from his current diet and onto the new food over a 7-day period. Observe stool quality. If the dog seems to be doing well, continue the game plan.

"Doing well" implies a number of things. First, it entails firm or formed stool. This may sound simple enough, but dogs with GI diseases can take quite a long time to show improvement. For our purposes, doing well means that the stool is not worse than before we started feeding the dog his new diet. With luck, you will notice some improvement soon, but do not be upset if this does not happen overnight. Signs of not doing well are vomiting or sloppier stool than before the new foods were introduced. If this should happen, remove the buckwheat and see if things improve when the dog is fed only buffalo meat. Since dogs can have a variety of responses to different kinds of fiber, buckwheat may need to be replaced with something else.

In this example, our hypothetical dog tolerates both foods. Once he has been fully weaned to the new diet, continue feeding it without supplements for one more week. Feeding 3 – 4 meals per day helps most of these dogs because their GI tracts are not overburdened trying to digest a large volume of food at once.

The next step is the addition of calcium. This diet provides the required amount of phosphorus, so dietary calcium alone is fine. Calcium carbonate is the generic calcium of choice if there is an abnormally high level of acid in the blood because it works as a buffering agent. For this dog, the goal is one half teaspoon of NOW® brand calcium carbonate powder per day. Start by adding only ¼ teaspoon daily, fed as ⅛ teaspoon twice daily mixed into food. Once stool inspection on the following day reveals that this amount is tolerated, repeat this amount for another two days. Calcium helps to make stool firmer. Our hypothetical dog is still doing well, and stool has firmed up a little, so start feeding the full amount of calcium, continuing to distribute it in two meals for another three days. Once the dog shows that this amount is tolerated, you can opt to feed the full calcium amount in one meal if you choose.

The easiest way of getting all vitamins and minerals into the dog is by feeding a multivitamin-mineral complex. Sometimes this works well, but with very limited diets like this one, and given the sensitivities of some dogs, I do not have many positive experiences with this method. Further, a multivitamin-mineral does not necessarily do a good job of keeping minerals balanced, and for small dogs like our 12-pound pooch, they can provide too much vitamin D. More often than not, I supplement vitamins and minerals one by one, noting the dog's reaction and moving forward with the diet plan as needed.

The only B vitamin that this diet provides enough of is niacin, so we need a vitamin B supplement. This can be provided in tablet or liquid form (children's vitamins are available in liquid form). Feeding B vitamins with food will prevent the nausea that these vitamins can create if fed on an empty stomach.

A few days of feeding a vitamin B supplement have gone by and the dog's stool still looks good, so we can move forward. The next step is to introduce one capsule of Allergy Research MultiMin™ per week. Tuck the whole capsule in a hand-held piece of food and feed it as a treat. Providing that stool quality over the next 48 hours remains good, this remains as a weekly addition.

At this point, the diet is low in copper, zinc, vitamins A and D. We can provide the correct amount of zinc by adding 15 milligrams of zinc citrate or gluconate weekly. This is usually tolerated best if fed in smaller amounts. Simply divide a capsule or cut a tablet in two and feed it twice weekly, mixed well into food.

We need an extra 1.5 milligrams of copper in the diet per week. You can find some chelated copper supplements in 1 milligram strength, so feeding 1.5 x this amount is easy. Add it to food, mix well and feed. Watch the stool and, assuming all goes well, we can begin to address the vitamin requirements.

Vitamin A can be provided by feeding vegetables high in carotene or by adding fish liver oil. Both are a little risky for dogs with GI disease because vegetables add fiber and oil adds fat. The advantage of cod liver oil is that it provides both vitamin A and D, so I try it first. In the diet for our theoretical dog, two cod liver oil capsules per week will provide enough of both vitamins. Since the diet provides only 8% of its kilocalories from fat, this small addition should not affect our dog — unless he is allergic to fish. In cases of PLE, even this tiny amount of oil could be a problem. Skip it if you need to. Plenty of direct sunlight will probably take care of the vitamin D requirement, and we could add a small amount of sweet potato or carrot to provide vitamin A.

If the dog continues to do well, now would be the time to try adding acidophilus, followed by a little oil that provides omega-3 fatty acids. Dogs with PLE may not do well with any additional oils, so you may not want to rock the boat in these cases.

Beware of Hype

Despite claims to the contrary, there is not one magical diet or any supplements that cure GI diseases. I have come across claims like this one "I fed my dog this way and used these supplements and he no longer has IBD." A confirmed diagnosis of a certain gastrointestinal disease can only be made after the dog has been scoped. It stands to reason then that the only way to confirm "cured IBD" would be to scope the dog again. Few if any veterinarians or pet owners would want this procedure performed on a dog that seemed healthy. So the word "cure" in this case is nothing more than an unsubstantiated claim. It may be correct to say that the dog no longer exhibits symptoms of IBD but "cure" is a very big word. I do not wish to minimize the importance that a given diet helped a dog, but *your* dog is a different being and could react in a very different way to the same diet.

Do not fall for claims of miracle diets. They simply do not exist. Do not buy into every supplement claim, and most importantly, do not spend your hard-earned money on a blend of powders that promise to provide great nutrition. Sensitive dogs can react negatively toward any of the ingredients in these formulations, and you would not know which ingredient created a problem. If you are living with a dog that has GI disease, you know that a setback can be serious. So why even go there? It is tough enough trying to get these dogs' GI tracts settled down when feeding simple diets, so stick to a plan and do not be swayed.

Chapter Summary

· IBD has been diagnosed in puppies and adult dogs.

· Mucosal inflammation disrupts normal absorption of some nutrients and can change motility.

· The immune system is involved in most cases of GI disease.

· Low-fat diets work best.

· Novel foods address the possibility of food allergies.

· Gut permeability is part of most GI diseases mostly because of the inflammation component.

· Most GI diseases are responsive to fiber.

· Diarrhea and vomiting can lead to dehydration and loss of water-soluble vitamins.

· Vitamin C can irritate the stomach and cause diarrhea.

· Sensitive dogs can react negatively to supplements as well as foods.

· Follow a step-by-step plan when introducing a new diet. Do not rush the process. It is important that you have enough time to note reactions to new foods and supplements.

· Feeding small, frequent meals helps dogs to digest food more easily. A dog that feels nauseous may better accept small meals.

· Beware of claims of cures for most GI diseases, and focus on control of symptoms and improved quality of life.

CHAPTER 20
Skin

Z ACH'S OWNER BRINGS HER DOG TO THE LOCAL ANIMAL SHELTER where she volunteers a few times every month. An underweight dog named McDuff was brought in a few weeks ago. Although some people thought he was rather homely looking, Zach seemed to think he was just fine. As a matter of fact, Zach started whining every time he had to leave his new friend. It did not take long before Zach and McDuff sat in the back seat of the car as if they had known each other their whole lives. McDuff was adopted into a forever home, and seemed to understand and trust the situation.

Once settled at home for a few days, McDuff's new owner noticed that the dog had very dry skin and he drank much more water than normal. Urinalysis and blood test results showed that he was healthy, but the veterinarian suggested that he had a fatty acid deficiency, probably due to being poorly fed.

The Fat and Water Connection

Many things, including disease and the moisture and/or fat content of a food affect a dog's water consumption. Healthy skin minimizes the migration of moisture upward from deeper dermal tissues. As we all know, oil and water do not mix. That is why the fatty acids in the skin do a good job of preventing water loss. In contrast, fatty acids deficiency can lead to a poor barrier, encouraging water loss. A dog may then drink more water to compensate.

The skin depends on food sources to provide essential fatty acids. McDuff may very well be suffering from a deficiency since he was thin when he arrived at the shelter, but overweight dogs can also have this problem. Feeding a large quantity of a poor quality food means the dog is receiving many calories, but not necessarily enough absorbable nutrients.

Protein

Most people think of protein as being necessary for healthy muscles but it is also a requirement for development of new skin. Some pet owners focus on the amount of protein being fed and while that is important, the quality of protein and digestibility should also be considered.

Most home-prepared diets provide ample high quality protein (fish, cheese, eggs, meat) but some are predominated by raw meaty bones. This is a questionable description because many foods can be classified as raw meaty bones. For example, chicken carcass provides little protein while a turkey thigh provides much more. Digestibility involves not only the production of a small, firm stool; but, more importantly, what actually happens inside the body after the food is consumed. For example, some of the protein content in RMBs comes from collagen. While this may sound healthy, collagen is broken down by bacteria in the bowel. A great deal of it is simply excreted when the dog defecates. Most RMBs provide a lot of fat. This may make a dog's skin and coat look quite lovely, but remember that high quality protein is required by the entire body and should also be a focus.

Vitamins

I have analyzed many home-prepared diets; and, surprisingly, many if not most are deficient in at least one B vitamin. Red meat is a good source of B vitamins but the word "good" is relative. It is certainly a better source than fowl or fish. However, a vitamin B deficiency can exist even when red meat makes up the majority of the diet. Some B complex vitamins act as cofactors in essential fatty acid metabolism.

One of the roles of vitamin A is maintenance of the upper layer of skin tissue. It is highly unlikely, but not impossible, for a home-prepared diet to lack vitamin A. While animal livers and liver oils provide ample vitamin A — sometimes too much — there are dogs with sensitivities or allergies to these items. Some dogs do not tolerate or will not eat enough of a vegetable that provides sufficient carotenes. In these cases, dietary supplementation with a multi-vitamin is necessary.

Vitamin E deficiency has not been reported to occur in dogs, but experimentally induced vitamin E deficiency does produce skin lesions.[36] Vitamin E works as an antioxidant. The appropriate amount to feed is based on the concentration of polyunsaturated fatty acids (PUFA) found in the foods we commonly feed our dogs. Because of their higher fat content, most meats, RMBs and eggs are good sources of polyunsaturated fatty acids. The need for vitamin E increases as PUFA increases.

Minerals

Mineral interactions can cause manifestation of skin problems. The most common problem I see is an excess of calcium, which in turn makes zinc less available. Foods high in calcium, phosphorus and magnesium are also a problem for the same reason. Zinc is responsible for many important functions, but more specifically to this chapter, it is an integral part of skin health.

There is a flip side to zinc: too much of it impedes copper absorption. Copper plays roles in skin and coat health, including pigmentation.

The source of minerals is key to absorption. Copper or zinc oxides are poorly absorbed. You may be thinking that this does not apply to you because you feed a home-prepared diet. This is only partially true. Many diets need the addition of a multivitamin or mineral complex. The forms of minerals matter, but it also goes beyond this. Vegetable sources of copper are not as well absorbed as meat sources. For instance, acorn squash provides quite a bit of copper compared to some other vegetables, but the copper is not as available to the dog as it would be if we fed beef liver.

We need to pay attention to the ratios between all minerals, but especially so in the case of copper, iron and zinc. These three interact based on how much of any are in the diet. A zinc to copper ratio of 10:1 is ideal. This will help skin health and positively affect other aspects of health.

36 Hand, M. S., Thatcher, C. D., Remillard, R. L., Roudebush, P. (2000) *Small Animal Clinical Nutrition,* 4th Edition.

Exceptions to The Rule

Some breeds prove that rules are meant to broken. Northern breeds tend toward a zinc malabsorption problem. Siberian Huskies and Malamutes are rather famous for this. Some owners automatically supplement with zinc because they feel this will avoid skin problems, but it is an ill-advised practice. More zinc than is necessary for a good diet can interfere with absorption of calcium and starts an avalanche of other mineral interactions. Extra zinc should be fed only under veterinary supervision.

Phytates are found in grains and vegetables. While most home-prepared diets do not provide nearly the phytate content that many commercial diets do, diets that address certain medical conditions such as pancreatitis can include plenty of grain or vegetables. Phytates make phosphorus, calcium, copper and zinc less available to the dog.

The health of the small intestine affects absorption of nutrients. Diseases that affect the small intestine leave it compromised, and malabsorption is not uncommon.

Dietary Guidelines

Unless there is an underlying health or genetic problem, skin health can return quite quickly simply by feeding a balanced diet. When they saw dry skin or coat, many of my clients began pouring oils into the food bowl. This helps in some cases but does not address possible vitamin and/or mineral deficiencies. Ultimately, the problem may diminish but never go away, or worse, the extra fat makes the skin and coat look better, and the dog owner does not look into the problem in more depth. In some cases, dogs will not consume additional oil or the diet the oil is added to. In others, the additional kilocalories increase body weight to an unacceptable level.

Skin is the largest organ of the body. Skin health can reflect what is happening on the inside of the dog as well. Be sure that the diet provides vitamins and minerals in the correct amounts, that minerals are in balance and in an absorbable form, and that sufficient essential fatty acids are being fed. You should see the first signs of skin improvement in about two weeks, six weeks maximum. Healing starts at the basal cell layer, so it can take awhile before changes are noticeable.

Chapter Summary

- Fatty acid deficiency results in a poor barrier, which encourages water loss. A dog may drink more water to compensate.

- The skin depends on food sources to provide essential fatty acids.

- Sufficient amounts of high quality proteins are required for skin health. Collagen is broken down by bacteria in the bowel, and a great deal of it is excreted when the dog defecates.

- Vitamins A, B and E are important for skin health. Vitamin C is critical for connective tissue health and formation since it is integral to collagen production.

- The amount of vitamin E to feed is based on the PUFA content of the diet.

- Interactions of minerals in an unbalanced diet can be the underlying cause of poor skin conditions.

- Siberian Huskies and Malamutes can have a zinc malabsorption problem.

- Never feed more zinc than necessary in a balanced diet without veterinary supervision.

- Phytates make zinc and other minerals less available.

- Diseases that affect the small intestine leave it compromised, and malabsorption is not uncommon.

- Unless there is an underlying health or genetic problem, skin health can return quickly simply by feeding a balanced diet.

- Skin healing starts at the basal layer and can take time to complete.

CHAPTER 21
Cancer

PERHAPS NO OTHER DIAGNOSIS STRIKES FEAR into our hearts the way that cancer does. Upon learning that their dog has cancer, most dog owners experience emotions ranging from denial to panic; and, finally, a heartfelt need for answers, including what to feed the dog.

Cancer research in animals and people has been going on for a very long time. Unfortunately, too little is known with certainty. Gregory Ogilvie, DVM, Dipl. ACVIM, is an internal medicine specialist and cancer researcher. Many of the diets and supplements on the Internet claim to be based on Dr. Ogilvie's research and/or recommendations of a diet that provides moderate, high quality protein, low carbohydrates and moderate to high amounts of fat, especially the omega or n-3 fatty acids such as docosahexaenoic acid (DHA) and eicosapentaenoic acid (EPA).

My goal for this chapter was to provide reliable information based on Dr. Ogilvie's own words. Only this can help us to ignore misinformation on chat lists and websites that stand to profit from using his name in order to promote a certain diet or supplement.

I had the pleasure of interviewing Dr. Ogilvie on November 10, 2006.

Q: *In your presentation about cancer at the WSAVA Congress in 2002, you stated "Fiber, both soluble and insoluble, is essential to maintain bowel health. A diet with adequate amounts of fiber is essential to prevent or to treat various problems of the gastrointestinal tract." Do you still feel this way, four years later?*

Dr. Ogilvie: Yes, absolutely.

Q: *At the same presentation, you noted that simple carbohydrates were best avoided. People seem to expand on this to say that all carbohydrates, including complex carbohydrates, should be avoided. Are you being misquoted?*

Dr. Ogilvie: Simple carbohydrates are generally not good and are often incorporated in modern over-the-counter pet foods because it is a relatively cheap ingredient and because it allows the formation of crunchy kibble or semimoist foods. Thus, from the food science point of view, it is desirable. It is in part responsible for health problems such as obesity, diabetes mellitus, dental disease and, perhaps, cancer. Certainly reduce carbohydrates but complex carbs are less of a concern.

Q: *There are many diets circulating the Internet that claim to be based on your findings and recommendations. Have you ever approved or suggested that any of these diets do indeed reflect a diet that you feel is healthy for a dog with cancer?*

Dr. Ogilvie: No. I have no problem with those that are based on science, however. I am not interested in recognition but I do not wish to be credited with misinformation.

Q: *Many people feed a raw diet to dogs with cancer. Your study included cooked foods only. Do you approve of raw diets?*

Dr. Ogilvie: The concept of raw diets is fine as long as they are truly fresh and they meet the nutritional needs of a pet, however they may have potential risk. Infectious agents can be a big problem. We've had, in this area, many dogs infected with salmon fever. This was from a raw food manufacturer who used contaminated fish. Now, if you ask would someone rather eat a frozen TV dinner or fresh foods — well, the answer is obvious. The spirit of the approach of raw feeding is good but the application is sometimes in error. The greatest problem may be that diets may not be nutritionally complete. Sources of nutrients are so variable.

Q: *Your trials included dogs that had lymphoma and were taking chemotherapy drugs. Have there been studies feeding this type of diet to dogs with other forms of cancer?*

Dr. Ogilvie: Yes. We have about 3,000 dogs and cats in clinical trials at the moment with and without chemotherapy, surgery and radiation therapy. The same positive results are seen.

Q: *Have you fed this type of diet to dogs that are not taking chemotherapy drugs and if so, what are the results?*

Dr. Ogilvie: Yes we have and the results are positive.

Q: *The current thinking is that you advise moderate protein, low carbohydrate, high fat diets, focusing on omega-3 supplementation. Are there more specific guidelines? For instance, you note that fat content (very low in omega-6 and high in omega-3) should make up 30 – 50% of kilocalories. This leaves us with 50 – 70% of kilocalories to be comprised of protein and carbohydrates. How much of each do you suggest?*

Dr. Ogilvie: This is not an easy question. Everyone wants a number, an answer, but it's not that simple. Carbohydrates are very bioavailable but protein varies. It depends on the bioavailability or digestibility of the protein.

Q. *Home-prepared diets usually provide high quality proteins from muscle meats and eggs; so in this case, would it be fair to say that 40 – 45% kilocalories from protein would be fine?*

Dr. Ogilvie: Yes.

Q: *Have you found any supplements whether through clinical trials or personal experience to be particularly helpful?*

Dr. Ogilvie: The diet should provide sufficient glutamine, cysteine and arginine, or should be supplemented with these. IP6 and CoQ10 may be helpful and some tumor types respond to Poly-MVA.

Q: *Have you made public any recommendations about supplements or a blend of vitamins that would legitimize claims stating the supplement is based on your recommendations?*

Dr. Ogilvie: No. We have, however, found that while supplementation with antioxidants such as vitamin E may be helpful at preventing cancer, it reduces the effectiveness of certain therapies and can diminish the effectiveness of DHA. Thus, more antioxidants is not better.

Q: *Most oncologists want the dog owner to stop supplementation of vitamins C and E when a dog is taking chemotherapy. Do you agree with this?*

Dr. Ogilvie: Yes. There is a good body of evidence that antioxidants should not be supplemented over the daily nutritional needs set by AAFCO.

Q: *Should a dog with cancer that is not taking chemotherapy be supplemented with vitamins C and E?*

Dr. Ogilvie: No.

Q: *Many people who own breeds prone to cancer are feeding this type of diet as a preventative step. Do you feel that this type of diet can prevent cancer in cancer prone breeds?*

Dr. Ogilvie: No diet has been proven to prevent cancer, however there are some important guidelines that have been proven. First and foremost, it is important that every dog remain lean throughout their entire life. Obesity has been shown to shorten life and to increase the risk of many diseases and disorders. Second, while n-6 fatty acids are essential for health and wellness, they should be reduced and an increase in omega-3 fatty acids is important. Carbohydrates increase the risk of obesity, insulin resistance and a tendency to develop diabetes and that, in turn, may increase the risk of developing many disorders and diseases, including cancer.

Q: *High amounts of omega-3 fatty acids have been associated with blood platelet coagulation problems. How do we reconcile this with the need to feed large amounts of n-3?*

Dr. Ogilvie: The amount of n-3 fatty acids is relatively small and thus, not associated with platelet or bleeding problems. While the amount of n-3 fatty acids that are used to treat cancer are higher, they have not been shown to be associated with health problems including platelet or bleeding problems.

Q: *The diet in your book, Managing the Canine Cancer Patient: Compassionate Care for Dogs with Cancer, does not state which brand of multi-vitamin/mineral.*

Dr. Ogilvie: We tried adding a number of brands that ended up being discontinued by the manufacturer. The book is also translated into different languages and different brands of vitamins aren't always available. A multivitamin and mineral supplement should be added as required to meet the AAFCO recommended allowance for dogs without exceeding the amounts for vitamins A, C and E.

Q: *The diet includes ground beef. What percentage of fat should this be?*

Dr. Ogilvie: The leanest available on the market and even then, the fat should be drained after the meat is cooked.

Q: *The diet includes rice. Is this whole grain brown rice?*
Dr. Ogilvie: Ideally, yes.

Q: *Do you consider this to be a diet suitable for life-long use?*
Dr. Ogilvie: It has been fed to dogs after treatment was completed and should be fine for long-term use.

End of interview.

Homemade Canine Cancer Food[37]
454 g (1 pound) lean ground beef, fat drained
227 g (1 ⅓ cups) rice, cooked
138 g (⅓ pound) beef liver
63 g (4 ½ tablespoons) vegetable oil
*9 g fish oil (nine 1000 milligrams fish oil capsules)**
*3.3 g calcium carbonate***
*2.9 g (¾ teaspoon) di-calcium phosphate****
1.9 g (⅓ teaspoon) salt substitute (potassium chloride)

This recipe will make 3 days' worth of food for a 25 – 30 pound dog. *Directions:* Cook the rice with salt substitute added to the water. Cook the ground beef and drain the fat. Cook the liver and dice or finely chop into small pieces. Pulverize the calcium carbonate and vitamin/mineral tablets. Mix the vegetable oil, fish oil (break open capsules), and supplements with the rice. Add the cooked ground beef and liver. Mix well, cover, and refrigerate. Feed approximately one third of this mixture each day to a 25 to 30 pound dog. Palatability will be increased if the daily portion is heated to approximately body temperature. *Caution:* when using microwave to reheat, avoid "hot spots" which can burn the mouth.

Nutrient Profile (% dry matter basis):
Protein 35.3   Sodium 0.36
Fat 41.6   Potassium 0.68
Carbohydrate 17.8   Magnesium 0.05
Calcium 0.65   Phosphorus 0.54
Energy 1,989 Kcal/kg as fed

---

37 Ogilvie, G. K. (2006). Recipe reprinted with exclusive permission.

Note: Owners are encouraged to feed the highest fish or preferably DHA oil dose tolerated by the dog.

**Calcium carbonate is available as oyster shell calcium tablets or Tums® (0.75 g. in Tums Extra®, and 1.0 g. in Tums Ultra®, GlaxoSmithKline).

***Bone meal can be used in place of di-calcium phosphate.

Author's note: A 2005 study[38] based on information gleaned from owner questionnaires, suggests strongly that there is a possible preventive effect against transitional cell carcinoma in dogs consuming green, yellow, or orange vegetables three or more times per week.

38 Raghavan, M., Knapp, D.W., Bonney, P.L., Dawson, M.H., Glickman, L.T. (2005) Evaluation of the effect of dietary vegetable consumption on reducing risk of transitional cell carcinoma of the urinary bladder in Scottish Terriers. *Journal of the American Veterinary Medical Association;* 227 (1): 94-100.

CHAPTER 22
The Senior Canine

M ANY YEARS HAVE PASSED. Our puppies grew into adults and enjoyed a variety of activities, lifestyles and canine friends. They have now entered their senior years. Their respective owners want to continue doing all they can for them. This includes feeding them the right diet for this stage of life, but they are not quite sure what that is. Should protein be restricted? Should phosphorus in the diet be reduced now that kidneys are older? Can arthritic changes be prevented with dietary changes or supplements? Will some of the dogs start to gain weight now that they are not as active as in their earlier years?

What's Really Happening?

An important change that occurs with age is that lean skeletal muscle mass decreases and body fat increases. Our dogs may look and even weigh the same as in the past, but the body mass composition has changed. Body strength depends on a combination of muscle mass, muscle tone and the integrity of the skeletal system. Physical strength lessens when muscle mass is less. As a result, dogs may be more lethargic or unable to do the work they previously did for as long a period of time. Most of the time, this makes for accelerated weight gain.

More weight and less muscle mass compromises the ability to move easily. Stress may be added to joints, heart and general body function. Digestive changes can also occur. For example, the body performs more efficiently when it is exercised, so, when exercise is reduced, some older dogs begin to have constipation problems.

Gender differences may have some impact. Females tend to accumulate more body fat than males as they go through the aging process. Breeds may also differ in their body fat-to-lean ratio.

Phosphorus

There is no reason to expect kidney function problems just because a dog is aging. Some dog owners are so concerned with trying to keep kidney disease away that they lower phosphorus in the older dog's diet. This is not necessary. In fact, decreasing the amount of dietary phosphorus can backfire. The healthy body continues to need phosphorus just as it always has. We create a phosphorus deficiency and a calcium imbalance if it is decreased too much.

Protein

The same concern about preventing kidney disease is what motivates some people to decrease the amount of protein in an older dog's diet. Do not let fear drive your decisions.

A study conducted by Purina notes that after three years, a higher mortality rate was seen in older dogs being fed a low protein diet (16.5%) compared to older dogs being fed a higher protein (34%) diet[39]. Although the mechanism of this effect is not well understood, it is hard to argue the results. There is no financial gain for a dog food company to state that an older dog needs a greater amount of protein.

Feed the dog, not the age of the dog. A healthy older dog does not require protein restriction. The majority of canine senior citizens continue to digest protein and fat without problems.[40] However, the older animal's gastrointestinal tract can become less efficient at digestion and absorption of protein and other nutrients, so we often need to load more into the diet for the body to take up its daily requirement.

Keep in mind biological value. Egg whites have the highest biological value, followed by milk, fish and meats. Every cell in the body needs protein. The cells of older dogs are no different. Feeding canine seniors high quality protein that is easily digested benefits the dog.

39 Kealy, R. D., (1999) Protein in Life Stage Nutrition – Factors Influencing Lean Body Mass in Aging Dogs. *Compendium on Continuing Education for the Practicing Veterinarian*; 21: 34-37.
40 Sheffy, B. E., Williams, A .J., Zimmer, J. F. and Ryan, G. D. (Apr 1985) Nutrition and Metabolism of the Geriatric Dog. *The Cornell Veterinarian*; 75(2): 324-347.

Calorie Restriction

While some older dogs continue to have high energy requirements, most slow down somewhat in their golden years. This is especially true if a dog has developed arthritis or other musculoskeletal problems (disc problems, dysplasia, etc.) over their lifetime. As a result, you will need to feed fewer calories to maintain a healthy weight. Some people simply feed less of the original home-prepared diet, but doing this also provides fewer amounts of nutrients. The dogs may need fewer calories per day but continue to need the same vitamin and mineral amounts as when they were younger.

The first step in reducing daily calories is to take a hard look at the treats you feed. Cutting back on them or changing the type of treat is sometimes all that is necessary. A dog that has been receiving baked goods such as high-calorie cookies can be given smaller bites. Give halves instead of wholes. Your dog will not notice the difference. Feed a green bean or baby carrot instead of a cookie at least once daily. Treats should be restricted to about 10% of daily caloric requirement.

Dogs that have been receiving beef marrow bones as chew treats can continue to have these, but scoop out the marrow beforehand. It is pure fat and adds a tremendous number of calories. Some dogs enjoy chewing and do not really care what they chew on. One of my own dogs thinks that a whole carrot is a great treat and makes a fun toy to roll around as well. At ten years old, she has a trim waistline. Part of that is due to feeding carrots rather than marrow bones.

Changing the Diet

In order to reduce calories further, we need to change the diet. This can be done in one of two ways. The first is to find leaner sources of protein. Chicken without skin is leaner than chicken with skin, venison is leaner than lamb, ground turkey is leaner than ground pork, and so on. The possible problem with this solution is that some food choices are less nutrient-dense than others. For example, chicken meat is a poor source of copper, iron, zinc and B vitamins. You would need to feed much more of it than venison, and even then, chicken simply does not provide the vitamin and mineral content most dogs need. While feeding greater amounts of a vitamin and mineral complex is one option, many people prefer to provide these nutrients in food sources.

VITAMINS	SOURCES
Vitamin A	Cod liver oil, animal livers
B vitamins	Beef, organ meats
Vitamin C	Fruits, vegetables
Vitamin D	Cod liver oil, canned salmon
Copper	Beef liver, canned oysters
Iron	Canned clams, beef heart
Magnesium	Fish, meats
Manganese	Brown rice, canned clams
Phosphorus	Meats, fish
Selenium	Chicken/turkey giblets
Sodium	Table salt, canned fish
Zinc	Canned oysters, beef, lamb
Potassium	Potato, sweet potato, squash, banana

Another way to go about the diet change is to search for more nutrient-dense foods. Some of the best choices are listed in the chart above.

Good sources of calcium and phosphorus include RMBs, bone meal and di-calcium phosphate. Turkey necks provide a great deal of calcium and phosphorus within fewer calories. Because of this, they can be an ideal substitute for high-fat RMBs. However, sometimes even this does not reduce calories sufficiently. In this case, use bone meal or di-calcium phosphate to provide calcium and phosphorus.

As you consider the nutrient-dense foods in the table above, remember to look at the USDA web site as you make changes in a diet. Simply feeding giblets to provide more selenium will not necessarily bring the nutrient values into balance. Giblets also add iron to the diet — potentially too much. It is just as easy to provide too much of a mineral as too little.

Red Meat – Friend or Foe?

Arachidonic acid is a fatty acid found in animal fat. It is important for healthy cell structure (membrane integrity) and for production of other prostaglandins that are important for life. Some of my clients with arthritic dogs worried when I added red meats to an arthritic dog's diet because they often read about a link between arachidonic acid and inflammation. None of the dogs I have ever worked with displayed problems in this regard. Perhaps this is because the information once presented on the Internet was, in fact, not based on the whole story. The visible fat portion of meat contains more arachidonic acid than lean the lean parts. Studies show that beef and lamb contain lower levels of arachidonic acid in both visible and lean portions than from other species. The highest level of arachidonic acid in both visible fat and meat are in duck. Pork fat has the highest concentration in the visible fat. The lean portions of beef and lamb contain higher levels of n-3 polyunsaturated fatty acids compared with white meats, which are higher in arachidonic acid and low in n-3.[41]

Supplements

Most diets need added vitamins and/or minerals. When we trim back calories, the need can be even greater. Review the new diet and take note of gaps that need to be filled. Find a multivitamin-mineral that will do the job or supplement with individual items as necessary.

Dietary fat remains an important player in the nutrition of older dogs. Most senior canines have some arthritis, so I avoid any oil that might add to inflammation. Commonly used oils such as corn, safflower and canola can add to the problem. I prefer to use a non-inflammatory version of omega-6 (primrose oil or borage oil) when a diet needs more of this essential fatty acid. Fish body oil, wild salmon oil being my personal favorite, provides omega-3 fatty acids and can help to reduce inflammation as well as being beneficial to the heart and compromised kidneys. Omega-3 fatty acids are taken up preferentially by the brain and skin as well.

Glucosamine products can be helpful to arthritic dogs. Some people say that chondroiten is useless because the protein molecule is too large to be absorbed, while others say it can benefit the dog. Chondroiten in the sulfate form is recommended for nutritional usefulness. MSM is also controversial. I have experienced the best results from high-quality products that contain all three ingredients.

---

41 Li, D., Ng, A., Mann, N.J., Sinclair, A.J. (Apr 1998) Contributions of meat fat to dietary arachidonic acid. *Lipids*; 33 (4): 437-40.

Advanced age can be accompanied by cognitive decline, which is indicative of central nervous system dysfunction. One possibly critical causal factor in this is oxidative stress. The Life Science department at the University of Toronto used canine models in an attempt to better understand the possible roles of dietary antioxidants:

"Old and young animals were placed on either a standard control food, or a food enriched with a broad spectrum of antioxidants and mitochondrial enzymatic cofactors. After 6 months of treatment, the animals were tested on four increasingly difficult oddity discrimination learning problems. The old animals learned more slowly than the young, making significantly more errors. However, this age-associated decline was reduced in the animals fed the enriched food, particularly on the more difficult tasks. These results indicate that maintenance on foods fortified with complex mixtures of antioxidants can partially counteract the deleterious effects of aging on cognition."[42]

Whenever possible, I use fresh foods to provide antioxidants. Fruits, especially berries and brightly-colored vegetables do this as well as making the dog feel full, which allows fewer calories to be fed. I have also added CoQ10 to the diet of many dogs. This is controversial because studies in dogs have not focused on CoQ10 for anything but heart disease, and the results were not impressive in that regard. However, clients continue to tell me that they see improvement in their older dogs. Is it because of the diet change alone or does CoQ10 play a role? Is this a case of the dog owner seeing want they want to see? I cannot say with certainty but I do give it to our 10-year-old dog Cassie. Although I may be doing nothing more than creating expensive urine, Cassie seems to be faring well.

Medical Changes

As discussed in previous chapters, addressing disease quickly is critical to longevity and quality of life. Most veterinarians agree that older dogs should have a check-up very six months. Remember that six months is at least 2 years in "people years." Many changes can occur during this period. Do you want to address kidney insufficiency early or wait until a dog is "suddenly" in renal failure? Do you want to address hypothyroidism now or wait until the thyroid is so exhausted that the

---

42 Milgram, N.W., Zicker, S.C., Head, E., Muggenburg, B.A., Murphey, H., Ikeda-Douglas, C.J., Cotman, C.W. (Sep-Oct 2002) Dietary enrichment counteracts age-associated cognitive dysfunction in canines, *Neurobiology of Aging;* 23 (5): 737-45.

whole body pays a price? The answers are obvious. We are fortunate to have the option of saving time and money or saving the dog. I have no doubt that you will choose the dog, so be sure to make that appointment with your veterinarian. Feel your dog's body for lumps and bumps before you go, mention any new behavior (more water consumption, a hesitancy to chew, less energy, etc.) and let the veterinarian decide what is or is not a health issue.

Chapter Summary

- With aging, lean skeletal muscle mass decreases and body fat increases.

- Less muscle mass equals less strength, and less strength equals less movement and usually weight gain.

- Females tend to have more body fat than males as they go through the aging process. Breeds may differ in their body fat-to-lean ratio.

- Most older dogs require fewer daily calories.

- Fewer calories can result in fewer amounts of nutrients. Feed nutrient-dense foods and a multivitamin-mineral or individual vitamins and minerals to address nutrient gaps.

- Neither protein nor phosphorus restriction is necessary due to age alone.

- Feed fewer, smaller and/or different types of treats to help restrict caloric intake.

- Red meats provide better nutrient profiles than fowl and do not necessarily provide more arachidonic acid.

- Non-inflammatory oils are better choices for arthritic dogs.

- Antioxidants may play important roles in cognitive function.

- Older dogs should be seen by their veterinarians every six months.

CHAPTER 23
Nutrient Requirements of Adult Dogs

I N 1985, THE NRC PRESENTED THEIR FINDINGS on the minimal nutrient requirements of dogs. In 2006, the much anticipated book, *Nutrient Requirements of Dogs and Cats*, became available. The book presented new guidelines, which upset some people who felt compelled to ask why the numbers have changed.

The simple answer is to say that we know more now than we did then. This should be reason to rejoice! Canine nutrition is not any different than human nutrition, in that we now have a better understanding of the increased need for calcium at certain stages of life, and that five to ten servings of fruits and vegetables daily are key to health.

Some people remain skeptical and email me to say so. Most emails look like this:

"I do not trust the numbers now! Why are the changes so dramatic? How can I trust the NRC when they've changed things so much?"

The changes we see are part of progress. The 1985 numbers were minimal requirements, whereas the 2006 numbers are recommended allowances. In other words, we do not want to either feed the bare minimum of a nutrient or reach toxic levels but rather, aim for optimal nutrition. This is achieved in steps. NRC 2006 is a big step forward to be sure!

A key point to consider is that, in reality, a dog's nutrient requirements are not linear with body weight. In other words, a dog weighing 100 pounds does not have the requirement of a 10-pound dog multiplied by 10. The new NRC numbers take this into consideration and give us a way of calculating recommended allowances so that we really can feed a dog as an individual.

To do this, we need to use a formula that may seem daunting at first glance. First, you need to know the dog's body weight in kilograms to the power of 0.75. Stay with me now! It is not as difficult as it sounds. If you are unaccustomed to metric weights and measures, take your dog's body weight in pounds and divide by 2.2 to arrive at kilograms. Calculating powers is not what most of us do for a living, so you will need a calculator to help you for the final step. The Microsoft® calculator in your computer system has the ability to calculate powers. Access this function by changing the view option to "scientific." The symbol to click is x^y. Other operating systems may have the same ability. If yours does not, many hand-held calculators have this ability. Key in your dog's body weight in kilograms. Press the x^y button followed by 0.75 and the = button. Congratulations — you did it!

The chart below shows Amt/kg BW/0.75. In plain English, this simply means the amount of a nutrient per kilogram of body weight to the power of 0.75.

The original table in the new NRC book also includes the amount of a nutrient per kilogram of dry matter and the amount of a nutrient per 1,000 kilocalories of metabolizeable energy. The majority of dog owners are not likely to work with these more complicated formulas. So, for the sake of simplicity, the table below shows only the amount of a nutrient per kilogram of body weight to the power of 0.75.

Note that some values are in grams (g). The USDA website notes some of the same values as milligrams (mg). Multiply one gram by 1,000 to arrive at milligrams.

Notes for the NRC table:

1. The quantity of tyrosine required to maximize black hair color may be about 1.5 – 2.0 times the quantity noted.

2. Some oxides of iron and copper should not be used because of low bioavailability.

3. Vitamin A expressed as RE (retinol equivalents). One IU (international unit) is equal to 0.3 RE. Safe upper limit values expressed as mcg retinol. One RE is equal to 1 mcg of all trans retinol.

4. One mcg of cholecalciferol = 40 IU vitamin D3.

5. Higher concentrations of vitamin E are recommended for high PUFA diets. One IU of vitamin E = 1 mg all d,l-a-tocopheryl acetate.

6. Dogs have a metabolic requirement for vitamin K but a dietary requirement has not been demonstrated when natural diets are fed. Adequate vitamin K is probably synthesized by intestinal microbes. The vitamin K allowance is expressed in terms of the commercially used precursor menadione that requires alkylation to the active vitamin K.

7. For normal diets not containing raw egg white, adequate biotin is probably provided by microbial synthesis in the intestine. Diets containing antibiotics may need supplementation.

8. In regard to n-3 fatty acids, eicosapentaenoic Acid (EPA) should be 50 – 60% and docosahexaenoic Acid (DHA) should be 40 – 50% of the total n-3 fatty acids.

Nutrient Requirements of Adult Dogs for Maintenance[43]

NUTRIENT	MINIMAL REQUIREMENT	ADEQUATE REQUIREMENT	RECOMMENDED ALLOWANCE	SAFE UPPER LIMIT
Crude Protein (g)	2.62		3.28	
Amino Acids				
Arginine (g)	0.092		0.11	
Histidine (g)	0.048		0.062	
Isoleucine (g)	0.098		0.12	
Methionine (g)	0.085		0.11	
Methionine & Cystine (g)	0.17		0.21	
Leucine (g)	0.18		0.22	
Lysine (g)	0.092		0.11	
Phenylalanine (g)	0.12		.015	
Phenylalanine & Tyrosine (g)	0.19		0.24	
Threonine (g)	0.11		0.14	
Tryptophan (g)	0.036		0.046	
Valine (g)	0.13		0.16	
Total Fat (g)		1.3	1.8	10.8
Fatty Acids				
Linoleic Acid (g)		0.3	0.36	2.1
a-Linolenic Acid (g)		0.012	0.014	
Arachidonic Acid (g)				
Eicosapentaenoic + Docosahexaenoic Acid (g)		0.03	0.03	0.37

43 *Nutrient Requirements of Dogs and Cats* (May 2006). Reprinted with express permission of the National Research Council (NRC).

Nutrient Requirements of Adult Dogs for Maintenance (continued)

NUTRIENT	MINIMAL REQUIREMENT	ADEQUATE REQUIREMENT	RECOMMENDED ALLOWANCE	SAFE UPPER LIMIT
Minerals				
Calcium (g)	0.059		0.13	
Phosphorus (g)		0.10	0.10	
Magnesium (mg)	5.91		19.7	
Sodium (mg)	9.85		26.2	
Potassium (g)		0.14	0.14	
Chloride (mg)		40	40	
Iron (mg)		1.0	1.0	
Copper (mg)		0.2	0.2	
Zinc (mg)		2.0	2.0	
Manganese (mg)		0.16	0.16	
Selenium (mcg)		11.8	11.8	
Iodine (mcg)	23.6		29.6	
Vitamins				
Vitamin A (RE)		40	50	2,099
Cholecalciferol (mcg)		0.36	0.45	2.6
Vitamin E (mg)		0.8	1.0	
Vitamin K (Menadione) (mg)		0.043	0.054	
Thiamin (mg)		0.059	0.074	
Riboflavin (mg)	0.138		0.171	
Pyridoxine (mg)		0.04	0.049	
Niacin (mg)		0.45	0.57	
Pantothenic Acid (mg)		0.39	0.49	
Cobalamin (mcg)		0.92	1.15	
Folic Acid (mcg)		7.1	8.9	
Biotin				
Choline (mg)		45	56	

CHAPTER 24
Other Diets

THE DIETS IN THIS BOOK tend to provide a variety of foods. There are simpler, faster ways of feeding your dog a fresh-food diet. The first is to use fewer ingredients. I have not provided these simple diets because, in my experience, few people want to feed that way. Show most people a diet that provides only ground beef and sweet potato and chances are they will tell me that their dog "needs" variety in the diet. The truth is that the dogs do not need variety because excellent nutrition can be had with very limited ingredients. Most dog owners feel a need to feed variety, so the diets in this book have been geared towards pleasing most people while providing the nutrition your dog needs.

Simpler diets also include a feeding method that uses Nature as the ultimate guide. "Whole prey" diets have become relatively popular. These are not something I would a call a diet plan per se. It is simply feeding a dog the entire prey animal. Of course, most dogs do not eat the entire prey animal in one meal. Instead, they are fed parts of that animal daily so that they consume the whole animal over a 1 – 2 week period. These diets would be better called "meat and bone diets" because none that I have seen are actually whole prey. The only thing they have in common is that they do not include vegetables, grains or supplements.

There are a few things to consider when choosing this method. First, because few of us have access to whole prey, we are unlikely to be able to buy a deer head, elk liver, and so forth. We are restricted to foods that are commonly available. Second, the nutrient content of farmed animals is vastly different from what a prey animal in the bush provides. Fat content may be more or less. Gut contents, and therefore B vitamins and some minerals, will be different between range-fed and grain-fed animals.

Third, most people who follow these diets feed lamb, turkey, beef and more; but these are not animals that roam freely in the wild. So we cannot consider them equal to the prey of a wild canid. Finally, a dog does not receive nutrients from uneaten foods, and small dogs would not be able to eat some parts, like a lamb's head, even it if was offered.

It is not my intent to offend anyone feeding a "whole prey" diet or to change your mind about feeding this way. Rather, I want to share two diets that are typical of what some of my clients feed, and to my mind, help you to improve the diet where necessary. As I stated earlier, I use the NRC guidelines because I cannot help a dog unless I apply nutrient values to the diet.

This diet was fed over a two-week period to a 62-pound, two year old dog that developed skeletal problems including arthritis.

Unbalanced Diet

6 ounces chicken carcass
24 ounces chicken quarters
2 ounces chicken neck
6 ounces chicken wings
2 chicken feet
16 ounces lamb rib
8 ounces lamb shank
16 ounces whole rabbit
8 ounces turkey neck
8 ounces turkey thigh
8 ounces turkey wing
1 turkey gizzard
1 turkey heart
1 turkey liver
16 ounces ground turkey meat
3 ounces lamb pancreas
4 ounces lamb spleen
8 ounces lamb tongue

10 ounces lamb meat (shoulder and leg)
4 ounces lamb brain
6 ounces lamb heart
7 ounces lamb kidney
3 ounces lamb liver
6 ounces lamb lung
16 ounces pork rib
2 pork ears
1 pork heart
2 pork kidneys
4 ounces pork liver
2 ounces pork tail
16 ounces ground pork meat
4 ounces pork tongue
2 large eggs with shells

This diet provides 970 kilocalories that break down as 40% from protein, 1% from carbohydrates and 59% from fat.

It provides more than 200% of calcium requirement, and almost as much extra phosphorus. While the zinc content is perfect on paper, excess calcium binds zinc, making it far less available to the body (interestingly, this dog had flaky skin that resolved 5 weeks after dietary changes). It contains only 50% of the magnesium requirement and 80% of the potassium requirement. The copper content is 95% of requirement.

While you may think that this is close enough, consider the days when a dog may not eat for one reason or another. Where is his copper reserve to help him out? Iodine is not supplied at all — sad news for the thyroid gland! Iron is 150% of requirement, which is a very risky level. Manganese, important for skeletal health, is less than 10% of requirement.

This second diet example was being fed to a 42-pound dog with a coat that was starting to fade from rich red tones to tan. He also had small, hard stools that were very difficult for him pass. He made this difficulty obvious by walking around the backyard in a hunched position, attempting to defecate.

His diet over a three-week period consisted of the following:

Unbalanced Diet

1 pound chicken giblets
1 pound chicken livers
1 pound chicken backs
1 pound chicken necks
2 pounds chicken wings
5 pounds chicken quarters
1 pounds pork ribs
1 pound ground pork
1 pound turkey necks
1 pound regular ground beef (30% fat)
6 large chicken eggs with shells

This diet provides 726 kilocalories per day that break down as 29% from protein, 1% from carbohydrates and 70% from fat.

Although it provides sufficient pantothenic acid, the diet is low in all other B vitamins. There is insufficient vitamin E. Calcium is provided at almost three times requirement, phosphorus just shy of double the requirement, and magnesium at about half of requirement. Sodium is provided at almost triple requirement, but this does not present a problem for healthy kidneys. Dietary potassium is half of what it should be. The diet provides no iodine. Iron is just shy of requirement, but copper is being provided at only 10% of what this dog needs. No wonder his coat lost so much color! There is less than 10% of required manganese, only 40% of required zinc, and about one third of required selenium.

As you can see, neither of these diets included supplements. This is true of all "whole prey" diets I have analyzed. The idea behind not supplementing is a belief that dogs do not need supplements of any kind. Where foods themselves provide all the nutrients a dog needs, this may be true. But as you can see, not all diets do this successfully.

Here is an example of a diet I formulated for a 50-pound dog that meets most of the ideology of a meat and bone diet. It also includes supplements and canned oysters to fill the nutritional gaps in the diet. This is where it swerves away from the basic ideology of raw meat and bone diets. I find that once a dog is in trouble, people will agree to use supplements, vegetables, or whatever it takes to make the dog feel better. Many nutrition-related problems can be avoided if the diet is improved sooner rather than later.

The following was fed over a two-week period:

Balanced Diet

29 ounces turkey thigh

6 ounces turkey wing

36 ounces ground beef, 15% fat

40 ounces beef heart

6 ounces beef liver

1 pound goat meat

8 ½ pounds ground turkey

5 large chicken eggs with shell

4 ¼ ounces canned oysters

25 milligrams vitamin B compound

1 ¼ teaspoons kelp

14 capsules, vitamin E 100 IU

25 milligrams manganese

1,500 milligrams magnesium

21,000 milligrams wild salmon oil

This diet provides 879 kilocalories per day and breaks down as 49% of kilocalories from protein and 51% from fat.

Why were these supplements necessary? Despite the amount of red meat in the the diet, it did not contain enough vitamins B1 and B2, so a vitamin B supplement filled the gaps. Kelp was used as a good source of iodine. A high fat diet like this one creates a greater need for vitamin E as an antioxidant. Grains are a rich source of manganese, but since the diet includes no grains, a supplement becomes necessary. A magnesium supplement was required in order to provide the dog with a better diet. Finally, wild salmon oil added omega-3 fatty acids.

Are you reading this and wondering where the wild canid finds his magnesium, B vitamins and more? Remember that no natural prey animal on earth is a combination of beef and turkey muscle meats attached to turkey RMBs and chicken eggs! Our modern meat and bone diets are not as natural as we might romanticize them to be. Even if they were, Mother Nature is not kind and nurturing. She does not care if a wild canid lives, reproduces, becomes ill or dies. She turns a blind eye to the hip dysplasia, arthritis, heart disease and other illnesses that wolves have been documented to have. On the other hand, dog owners want a long-lived and healthy dog. Using dietary supplements to improve the nutrient profile of a diet is a much better plan than hoping we can outrun diet-related health issues by feeding a variety of foods.

Chapter Summary

- A proactive approach means considering NRC values before a dog is ill.

- Good nutrition can be provided by feeding simple diets that contain few ingredients or by feeding a greater variety of foods.

- "Whole prey" diets rarely provide natural prey animals but rather, many body parts of a variety of farmed animals.

- Animals raised by man, whether in lot farm settings or on more natural pastures, do not have the same nutrient profile as animals in the wild.

- A dog does not receive nutrients from unconsumed foods such as the jaw of a sheep, the head of an elk, etc.

- Meat and bone diets may require supplementation in order to meet NRC recommendations, and while these recommendations may not be acceptable to some people, they can help to guide us once a dog is ill.

- Mother Nature is not interested in the lifespan, reproductive ability or health of animals.

CHAPTER 25
Herbs and Natural Remedies

I WAS BORN IN ROMANIA and came to Canada at five years of age. At that time, Romania did not have much in the way of drugs to treat some major illnesses, much less smaller problems like diarrhea, rashes and other common childhood issues. My mother was left to treat and cure many ailments in the same way that her mother and grandmother had, with natural remedies and herbs.

My mother's natural cures did not change once we arrived in Canada. She saw no need to change what she was doing because it usually worked well and she knew her limitations. Persistent or high fever, serious pain or ongoing diarrhea meant we were going to the doctor. Actually, in those days it meant the doctor could come to us too, because at the risk of dating myself, family doctors used to make house calls!

Brewed mint tea was used to stop diarrhea. Chamomile tea was used to calm an upset stomach. Witch hazel compresses were applied to bruises. Warm salt-water gargles helped to soothe an irritated throat. Cod liver oil was given during the winter if several days of dark skies or inclement weather prevented me from playing in direct sunlight. I can still remember running as fast as my feet would carry me away from the teaspoon with the horrid tasting oil.

Rashes that my mother had decided were due to contact with some kind of plants were treated with oatmeal compresses. Head and chest colds were treated by adding some eucalyptus to a pot of boiling water. Mom would place the pot on a table and a towel over my head so I could inhale the fragrant steam. It made my hair frizzy and my face wet but I could breath well throughout the night. I did not know that nasal spray existed, nor did I need it.

Perhaps it is because herbs and natural remedies were used only when I was feeling unwell that I always looked upon them as being medicinal. My mother never gave me mint tea as a drink. I may not have thought of mint as being particularly special if she had. Instead, my reaction to its potent ability to stop diarrhea so quickly was no different than another person's would be to an over-the-counter product that did the same thing. Just as that child would not become an adult who took over-the-counter products on a whim, I grew up respecting herbs and natural remedies for what they are — medicinal.

My respect for herbs extends to the possibility of interactions between herbs themselves and between herbs and prescription medicines. I continue to use teas and some natural remedies, just as my mother did, to address certain heath problems.

Today, the medicinal properties of herbs have been proven time and again. Milk thistle (Silybum marianum) is a prime example. With so many studies showing its benefits for the liver, traditional medicine has embraced it to the point where it has become almost standard protocol. However, as with almost everything else in life, there is a downside to herbs and the way they are marketed.

Pharmacies, health food stores and specialty herb markets have turned these medicines into an over-the-counter purchase. There was a time when herbs were used with respect, but for many people, that time has passed. Herbs are discussed on Internet chat lists as if we were talking about how much sugar should be added to a cake recipe. A question is asked and the replies vary: Yes, use it throughout the year; no, use it only when there is an ailment; use it once per month; use it only during its natural growing season...and the advice goes on. So, are there rules about herbs?

I am not an herbalist or a veterinarian. In my opinion, these are the people we should be asking, especially the veterinarian. However, there are still pitfalls in regard to asking about the use of herbs. The first is that not all veterinarians know enough about herbs to be able to prescribe them. The second is that we tend to ask questions of people who are most likely to tell us what we want to hear.

Some clients ask me to tell them about an herb or food that will kill intestinal worms. They do not want to use chemicals. They want to use something natural. Many of today's drugs were derived from plants, so we have to ask: if the drug has some toxicity level, why not the plant it is derived from? Black walnut is said to get rid of worms, but it can be toxic to the dog in addition to the worms. What we do to the host of a parasite needs to be balanced with the risk of doing nothing, or using a prescription drug or an herb.

Even "safe" herbs and remedies can cause problems. Oatmeal shampoo may sound natural and soothing, but use it on a dog that is allergic to oats and chances are that you will not like the outcome. Add chamomile tea (some people do this in an effort to calm the digestive tract of their dog) to the food of a dog that is allergic to ragweed, and the dog may end up at the veterinary emergency clinic.

Belief Systems vs. Reality

While I believe in using herbs and natural remedies at times, I also know that they are not always the best option. For example, a client of mine fed her dog garlic, brewer's yeast and apple cider vinegar to keep fleas away. She insisted that this was working because her dog never had fleas — until now. I did not feed any of these things to our Zoey, and she never had fleas even once. But that is neither here nor there. The more important part of this story is that this client truly believed that flea prevention was based on certain foods and supplements. When the dog proved her wrong, she wanted to boost his immune system because she had read that parasites are more attracted to a compromised body. To this end, she omitted all grains and vegetables from the dog's diet, added vitamin C, increased the amount of vitamin E and started adding a powdered blend advertised as being able to improve the immune system. The result was that the house became flea infested to the point that the person had to move out while it was being sprayed. The poor dog became not only the fleas' food source, but also contracted tapeworms from the flea infestation and calcium oxalate urinary crystals from an unbalanced diet (which is why I began working with his owner).

This next example shows us that even when herbs are a wonderful choice, quality is key. Like other plants grown for sale, herbs can be treated with chemicals to safeguard them from pests. Organically-grown herbs may be of better quality in this regard. Still, contamination can come from water or air as the sprays from neighboring farms enter the environment. Herbs can be dried through chemical processes or picked and dried naturally. In either case, improper drying can result in yeast and mold. Yeast and mold are part of nature and not usually something to worry about, but a high mold count can cause negative reactions in some dogs. This was the case for a dog that had elevated liver enzymes.

The owner purchased milk thistle at a good price from a store that sold herbs in bulk. The dog began to scratch himself at all hours of the day and night. While he might have been allergic to the herb itself, I was suspicious about the quality. Since at that time, I was looking for a high quality milk thistle and sending samples to the lab to test for mold counts, I offered to send a sample of her milk thistle to the same lab. Sure enough, the mold count was very high. It took almost two weeks before the dog stopped scratching after the original product was discontinued.

Quality is key and laboratory findings are important to consider. As with other supplements, you should be able to see a laboratory assay upon requesting one from a supplier. Having your request turned down speaks for itself.

Claims vs. Facts

Sometimes the claims about herbs are factual but incomplete. For instance, some websites, especially those that sell alfalfa, tell us that this herb contains all known vitamin and minerals. While this information may be valid, it fails to mention the amounts of vitamins and minerals and how this compares to a dog's requirements. Alfalfa fails the test in this regard because we would have to feed pounds of it daily in order to come remotely close to mineral requirements. This does not make it a bad food, but neither is it a magical ingredient.

Probiotics are the good-guy bacteria residing in the gut. We feed probiotic supplements with the hope that the viable organisms will establish themselves and flourish. Acidophilus is the best-studied probiotic in dogs and the one that I personally use. If you think that all probiotics are healthy for your dog, consider a study showing that a strain of E. faecium actually increased the gut population of Salmonella spp. and Campylobacter spp.[44]

Dogs vs. People

Despite that some people call them "furbabies," dogs are not little people with tails. They are a different species. The results of studies conducted in test tubes, on other animals or on people may not apply. Although there are some reasonable websites that discuss the possible benefits and

---

44 Vahjen, W., Manner, K. (Jun 2003) The effect of a probiotic Enterococcus faecium product in diets of healthy dogs on bacteriological counts of Salmonella spp., Campylobacter spp. and Clostridium spp. in faeces. *Archiv für Tierernährung*; 57 (3): 229-33.

toxicities of herbs and natural remedies, it is important to know where the information comes from. If the site discusses herbs as they relate to human diseases and reactions, remind yourself that the same substance or food may be ineffective for dogs or, worse, might cause a serious reaction. Examples of this are Heinz body anemia in dogs that eat onions, or the fact that chocolate is toxic to dogs. Reactions to foods and herbs can be very different and deserve consideration.

Chapter Summary

- Herbs are medicines and may have benefits as well as toxicities associated with them.
- Yeast and mold are part of nature and thus part of what an herbal preparation may contain.
- Laboratory assays should be made available to the purchaser of supplements and herbs.
- Some claims may be factual but incomplete.
- Some claims do not apply to dogs.
- Some natural substances may be detrimental rather than beneficial.
- Consult a veterinarian before feeding herbs.

CHAPTER 26
Optimal Nutrition

THE GREATEST LESSON THAT OUR ZOEY TAUGHT ME is that what other people think is optimal nutrition for dogs may not be. Not for her, and not for any dogs I have worked with. While certain dietary rules apply in cases of disease, every dog responds differently.

Zoey was my learning dog and she taught her lessons well. I had just finished writing my first book and was happily announcing her varied diet when she had another major colitis flare up. She took the meaning of a fiber-responsive condition to an extreme. In theory, eleven ounces of squash per day for a 19-pound dog should produce soft stools, but not for Zoey. This, combined with three ounces of turkey, kept her little gut happy right to the end.

You have your own learning dog(s). Each has at least one important lesson, and all will show you that optimal nutrition is based on much more than being emotionally attached to a certain feeding method. In some cases the challenge will be greater because you may need to address a nutritionally-responsive disease in a dog that does not necessarily tolerate the foods or feeding method you think is best. Be patient.Let the facts guide you, but follow your dog's lead as well.

When we are feeling overwhelmed, we sometimes forget to lift our eyes off the pages of a book or the computer screen and look at the dog instead. The dog is what matters. Cooked diets, raw diets, combination diets — any of these might be considered optimal for a given dog. The formulation of a diet is ultimately based on the dog owner's comfort level with a particular method of feeding and the dog's tolerance level of that choice.

Appendix

List of Recipes

List of Charts

Index